S0-BYI-542

Joint Ventures in the Soviet Union

IV

Joint Enterprise Foreign Economic Activities

1. Joint Enterprises in Production Cooperation

Economic cooperation in various forms has become a common phenomenon among enterprises from different countries. Such cooperation is especially significant for numerous countries in advancing their economies, not least because it serves them in attaining heightened levels of science, technology and production. Cooperation can also yield considerable material gains, while, at the same time, since it helps to advance new branches in science and technology, boosting and modernizing production without any additional expenditure, on the basis of partners' achievements.

Cooperation is characterized by stable, and usually long-term contacts between partners that can bring about even closer relationships and, in some instances, lead to joint enterprises, international amalgamations and organizations with different institutions, firms and management bodies from the participating countries. Such entities are often referred to in academic literature as joint economic organizations (JEOs) and joint enterprises (or JEs). *(editor's note: the JE has been a form of economic cooperation among CMEA countries. The CMEA no longer exists as an intergovernmental organization, although economic relations among former CMEA countries continue albeit at different levels.)*

A shift from simple to more complex forms of cooperation is typical of economic integration. To exemplify one example, we might consider the Soviet-Bulgarian research and production machine-tool amalgamation Karat-Pooldarv-Barac.

On 27 June 1969, the CMEA countries signed the *Agreement to establish, on a permanent basis, a joint specialized production* of flexible machine-building systems and their extensive use in the national economies. In October that year, the Soviet and Bulgarian

JOINT VENTURES IN

THE SOVIET UNION

General editor
M. M. BOGUSLAVSKII

English edition edited with commentary by
M. M. BOGUSLAVSKII
and
T. J. STUBBS

Introduction and legislative texts by
W. E. BUTLER

I.B.Tauris & Co Ltd
Publishers
London · New York

Published in 1992 by
I.B.Tauris & Co Ltd
110 Gloucester Avenue
London NW1 8JA

In association with Nauka Publishers, Moscow

175 Fifth Avenue
New York
NY 10010

In the United States of America
and Canada distributed by
St Martin's Press
175 Fifth Avenue
New York
NY 10010

Copyright © 1992 by Nauka Publishers
English language edition © 1992 by I.B.Tauris & Co Ltd
Appendices © 1992 by W.E.Butler

All rights reserved. Except for brief quotations in a review, this book, or any part
thereof, must not be reproduced in any form without permission in writing from the
publisher.

A CIP record for this book is available from the British Library

Library of Congress catalog card number: 91-68015
A full CIP record is available from the Library of Congress

ISBN 1-85043-200-7

Contents

Preface

The appearance of this volume has a distinctive history of its own. Originally it appeared in a Russian language and several foreign language versions as part of a popular social sciences multilithed series of limited circulation issued by Nauka, the Publishing House of the Russian (then USSR) Academy of Sciences.

The original English version (which was not done by the original Soviet authors) has been sympathetically reworked first, in part, by Mr. W. B. Simons, of the Documentation Office for East European Law, University of Leiden, and in its present form by Professor M. M. Boguslavskii and Mr. T. Stubbs, JD (Michigan), an Associate with Cole Corette & Abrutyn (London and Moscow). Responsibility for that text belongs to them.

The element of obsolescence Messrs. Boguslavskii and Stubbs have dealt with by interpolating Editorial Notes and Comments at appropriate places in the footnotes or at the end of the Chapters.

The texts of legislation appended, on the other hand, are translated by myself, and for them I assume full responsibility.

London, 1 January 1992   W. E. Butler

Editorial Introduction

We customarily associate perestroika with the coming to power of Mikhail Gorbachev in March 1985, and not without reason. The economic dimension of perestroika, however, truly commenced some 17 months later with the enactment of two decrees, still not published in full, on 19 August 1986. Their existence was not publicly disclosed until 24 September of the same year, when the Soviet press carried a brief announcement indicating that joint enterprises with foreign participation might be created on the territory of the USSR.

Although these two decrees were lengthy and introduced a number of measures, joint enterprises rightly received the most attention because of their revolutionary import: it meant that foreign equity ownership in a Soviet corporate entity was possible for the first time in nearly six decades. The decrees represented another round of economic reform in an economy which seemed perpetually to be the object of tinkering, but unusually in this case because the reform commenced by addressing foreign economic relations rather than, as so often previously, leaving this dimension of economic behaviour either untouched or until the last.

From the conditions associated with the creation of joint enterprises – these were elaborated in an edict and Decrees Nos 48 and 49 adopted on 13 January 1987 – it was evident that the new policies were experimental and tentative. Foreign participation was sought, of course, but so was foreign reaction – itself something new in foreign economic relations. The architects of the new policies hoped that in the course of time foreign equity investment would bring much-needed hard currency, modern technology, a competitive example for the domestic economy to emulate, enhanced exports, import substitution, as well as, in the medium term increased employment, a more highly skilled labour force, increased supplies of consumer goods and a higher standard of living. Ultimately the Soviet Union was to become integrated with the world market economy, have a fully convertible currency and assume its proper role as a major economic player in the international arena.

This has been an economic strategy from the outset conceived as part of a larger socio-political and legal strategy. Perestroika, in the minds of its creators, could not succeed without new thinking, glasnost, and social, political and legal reforms of no less magnitude. Integration with the world economy meant the dismantling of thoroughly discredited state planning, management, and political structures, a reordering of relations between the centre and the republics, and a return to the mainstream of international law and relations. By 1992 the Union of Soviet Socialist Republics had been reformed into a species of confederation with a smaller constituency, a vastly attenuated central authority, and into an economic community which resembled more an international organization than a classic state structure. Amidst, and as part of, these political and legal reforms the commitment to a market economy intensified and the true legal measures required to implement that strategy began to unfold.

It is instructive to look back at some of the principal benchmarks. The novelty of allowing and encouraging foreign equity ownership on Soviet territory as from January 1987 was accompanied by a number of requirements that made such investment less than attractive: a minimum Soviet share of 51 per cent, certain nationality conditions for executives of joint enterprises, and a number of analogous provisions. These were modified in the course of months, but the joint enterprise remained for some time a corporate entity *sui generis* under Soviet law, with the foreign investor being offered inducements to invest that were largely exceptions not merely to the national regime, but to a regime that favoured the continuance of a centrally planned economy. Investors were naturally cautious as they looked behind the original inducements and considered with care what would truly be involved in commencing operations within the Soviet economy.

'Joint enterprise', which originally came to mean Decree 49 JE, gradually broadened conceptually to encompass almost any kind of joint investment in a corporate entity, including only by Soviet parties. 'Joint ventures', of course, are even broader, embracing contractual non-corporate schemes of almost infinite variety. In 1990 the first generation of Soviet corporate legislation arrived: a law on enterprises, a statute on joint-stock societies and limited responsibility societies, and signals that sundry forms of partnership were in the offing. The joint enterprise suddenly became obsolescent, except insofar as specific economic privileges were conferred by the original contracts, and most foreign parties, after an edict of the President of the USSR on October 1990 clarified the position, began to opt for traditional stock-issuing entities. An embryonic securities market began to form – it paradoxically being easier to create banks and stock exchanges under Soviet law than many other types of entity – and the rudiments of a market economy to emerge.

Implicit in all of these reforms, however 'liberal' or 'permissive' they become, is some type of authorization procedure for the foreigner to become part of the Soviet economy. Usually this takes the form of registrations of various kinds. At the beginning a joint enterprise proposal for registration had to be accompanied by a substantial feasibility study and a host of clearances or approvals by superior agencies. Gradually these have either become a pure formality or been eliminated. Free and direct access to the Soviet market, however, has been resisted to the end.

A major benchmark in this connection is an edict of the President of the Russian Soviet Federal Socialist Republic (RSFSR) liberalizing foreign economic relations, adopted on 15 November 1991. The edict in effect gives citizens and legal persons alike direct access to the foreign market with what promise to be the most elementary and purely routine procedures required; the corollary should be equivalent access to the Russian domestic market on the part of foreign firms. In pursuing a market philosophy in law reform, there are several further benchmarks to be consolidated during 1992:

1. The introduction of legislation on pledge which fully enables Soviet legal and natural persons to deploy their assets and assume risks. Perhaps no legislation is more fundamental to attracting foreign investment and unleashing the entrepreneurial powers of the domestic economy.

2. The registration of branches of foreign companies in Russia and other republics. A branch is not a juridical person under Russian law. There are many reasons why a foreign company may wish to create a branch on Russian territory, including taxation, but from the perspective being explored here the key is whether foreign business activity may take place in the Russian Federation without the formality of creating a separate legal person. As this becomes accepted, the pace

of foreign involvement in the Union and republic economies is likely to accelerate substantially.

3. The clarification of issues of ownership that enable state agencies and other owners or possessors of assets to pass clear title to acquirers.

Most of the first-generation market economy legislation is in place in the republics. Truly largescale foreign investment in natural resources exploitation, privatized enterprises, tourist and transport infrastructure, manufacturing where appropriate and high technology will come with the second-generation law reforms, the polishing of the initial legislation and the enactment of the secondary level of detailed normative enactments needed to flesh out what is, on the whole, still a rudimentary legal framework.

The Union and economic community dimensions of the equation will require time to mature and gestate, but each will have legislative competence in some degree. Bilateral and multilateral treaties – in the broadest sense of the term – will have a substantial regulatory role at least in the short and medium terms. The 'war of laws' between the centre and the republics may degenerate into a war of laws amongst the republics on occasion, and whatever the scenario the foreign investor will encounter at least two new strata of regulation: the economic community and the inter-republic treaty.

Much of the material in the chapters that follow is already history, but instructive history at that. To understand where Russia is proceeding, or likely to proceed, one must comprehend where she has been in the immediate past. Some of what happens will be a response, a reflex, against what has been. The balance will be new, hopefully an intelligent adaptation and blend of domestic experience and foreign example that will bring the Russian legal system into a market economy at the forefront of standards of the twenty-first century.

W. E. Butler

Introduction

The work we offer to our readers' attention deals with various aspects of the establishment and operation of joint enterprises (JEs) with foreign participation on the territory of the USSR. The formation of the economic and legal prerequisites for the creation in the Soviet Union of such enterprises is one of the elements of perestroika currently under way in the national economy and the transition to a market economy.

Measures aimed at the fundamental improvement of the management of foreign economic activity and economic and scientific–technological cooperation with foreign countries are part of the basic restructuring of the economic mechanism in the USSR, which began with resolutions of the 27th Congress of the Communist Party of the Soviet Union (CPSU).[1]

Speaking in London at the Guildhall in April 1989, Mikhail Gorbachev stated that perestroika in the Soviet Union was a serious and long-term programme, and that this programme assumed a deeper involvement of the USSR in the world economy. He added that recognition of such factors as the interdependence of states and the USSR's attempts to enter rapidly into existing economic relationships and to integrate into the world economy had led to the necessity of establishing a qualitatively new mechanism for foreign economic affairs.

Soviet governmental decisions on the possibility of establishing JEs with foreign participation on the territory of the USSR were adopted in August 1986. The Soviet government acknowledged the expediency of developing in every possible manner the external economic activity of Soviet enterprises on the basis of the Law of the USSR on the State Enterprise (Association) of 30 June 1987. This law unambiguously provided for the participation of Soviet enterprises in joint enterprises

(Art. 19, para. 2). In accordance with changes and amendments to the Law on the State Enterprise introduced by a law of 3 August 1989, state enterprises were permitted, *inter alia*, to establish associations or consortia with joint enterprises.

The Law on the State Enterprise provides that an enterprise shall enter into economic relations with foreign firms on the principles of mutual benefit and equality, and that the main forms of developing such relations are long-term and balanced production and scientific–technological cooperation, as well as the establishment of joint enterprises (Art. 19, para. 3).

Decree No. 1074 of the Central Committee (CC) of the CPSU and the USSR Council of Ministers of 17 September 1987 provides for measures aimed at further developing cooperation with firms from foreign countries and streamlining the operation of joint enterprises. In pursuing the consistent implementation of the course to utilize the advantages of the international division of labour, it was acknowledged as expedient to intensify significantly the cooperation of ministries, departments, associations and enterprises in promoting cooperation with capitalist and developing countries, an integral part of which was the establishment of joint enterprises.

The adoption of the Law on Cooperative Societies in the USSR of 26 May 1988 opened up new wide vistas for setting up joint enterprises. This law was aimed at speeding up Soviet scientific–technological progress and increasing the competitiveness of Soviet products and services. The law granted cooperatives engaged in production activity the right to set up joint enterprises with firms and organizations from any foreign country.

Cooperatives, in agreement with foreign partners, were given the power to determine JEs' specialization, the volume and structure of their production, taking into account the demand for their products (goods or services), and the terms of marketing, including prices. Joint enterprises were allowed to be established both on the territory of the USSR and overseas. In December 1988 the Soviet government took additional measures to attract further foreign capital to set up JEs in the USSR.

What is a 'joint enterprise'? In Soviet legal literature on the subject,[2] a joint enterprise has been defined most often as a comparatively new form of international economic cooperation. But it is undoubtedly a far more complex form than normal cooperation of this type between domestic enterprises, since it is directly linked with international production and other cooperation. A joint enterprise is characterized by such elements as common property, joint management and joint participation in distribution of profits and losses. In this sense the joint enterprise may be compared to the Western 'general partnership' or 'closely held corporation'; but as an entity organized under Soviet law the JE is distinct in a number of important respects. A joint enterprise is regarded as a *collective formation* built upon the membership of economic firms or organizations of *two or more countries* with a view to carrying out *joint economic activity*. It possesses distinct property made up of the initial contributions of its partners and income received by the joint enterprise itself; it operates on the principles of economic accountability and is a legal entity (or 'juridical person') in accordance with the laws of the country of its situs (or 'host country').[3]

In the present publication a joint enterprise is understood to be a Soviet legal entity established on the territory of the USSR, formed on the basis of an agreement between two or more parties in accordance with Soviet legislation. The parties to the JE are subjects of the laws of various states. The JE engages in production, scientific-technological and other economic activity both in the USSR and abroad, possesses distinct property and is independently liable for its obligations.

The concept 'joint enterprise' should be distinguished from the concepts 'international association' and 'joint organization', which terms have in the past been used in Soviet legislation to identify the forms of cooperation among the countries of the Council for Mutual Economic Assistance (CMEA or Comecon).

International associations were set up to coordinate production, scientific-production and other economic activity carried out by their participants in industry, science, agriculture, civil engineering, trade, transport and other sectors of the national economy. Such associations were established on the principle of retention of national ownership of the participants' property. Where necessary the participants partially combined their property to engage in economic activity.

Joint organizations (research and development, design and construction, etc.) were set up to carry out research and development, design and construction and other activity on the basis of common socialist property.

Thus the nature of activity serves as the criterion for identifying joint enterprises and joint organizations. This publication does not deal with matters pertaining to international associations and joint organizations.

To resolve the issues arising from the establishment of joint enterprises in the USSR and to ensure their normal operation, the appropriate legal basis and legal regulation have been seen as necessary. The 'centre of gravity' of such regulation in each country has been its own domestic law.

What should be considered as the sources of legal regulation in this matter? We would draw the reader's attention to special normative acts and special legislation. One relevant act was the Edict of the Presidium of the USSR Supreme Soviet of 26 May 1983, 'On the procedure for the activity of joint economic organizations of the USSR and other CMEA member countries on the territory of the USSR' (the Edict of 1983). However, this act dealt exclusively with joint economic organizations between CMEA member countries.

Subsequently, beginning in 1987, the principal legislative acts pertaining to joint enterprises were adopted. These included:

1. The Edict of the Presidium of the USSR Supreme Soviet of 13 January 1987, 'On questions connected with the creation on the territory of the USSR and the activities of joint enterprises, international associations and organizations with the participation of Soviet and foreign organizations, firms and agencies of administration' (the Edict of 1987);[4]

2. Decree No. 48 of the USSR Council of Ministers of 13 January 1987 'On the establishment on the territory of the USSR and activities of joint enterprises, international associations and organizations of the USSR and other CMEA member countries' (Decree 48);[5] and

3. Decree No. 49 of the USSR Council of Ministers of 13 January 1987, 'On the procedure for the creation on the territory of the USSR and the activities of joint enterprises with the participation of Soviet organizations and firms of capitalist and developing countries' (Decree 49).[6]

(*Editor's note.* As of 1992 the above acts had been substantially supplemented by new legislation on entrepreneurial activities, foreign investments, new Soviet company laws at the all-Union and republic levels and other legislative developments; see, for example, Appendices 2 and 3.)

Substantive provisions regarding the organization and operation of joint enterprises are provided for in Decree No. 1405 of the USSR Council of Ministers of 2 December 1988, 'On further development of foreign economic activity of state, cooperative and other social enterprises, associations and organizations'.

Alongside these fundamental acts, various agencies (including the USSR Ministry of Finance and the USSR State Committee for Supplies) adopted a range of normative acts regulating certain matters of the operation of joint enterprises (for example, the procedure for their registration, taxation, material and technical supplies, etc.).

In a given instance sources of legal regulation may also include international agreements. Both Decree 48 (para. 3) and Decree 49 (para. 1) state that joint enterprises shall be guided in their activities by the laws of the USSR and the Union republics except as otherwise provided for in international treaties (see also Appendices 2 and 3).

Of particular importance for the establishment of joint enterprises are bilateral treaties of the Soviet Union concerning the mutual protection and promotion of investment. Such treaties have been concluded with Great Britain, France, the Federal Republic of Germany, Belgium and others. These contain provisions providing for payment of compensation in the event of nationalization or requisition as well as guarantees regarding repatriation of profits (see *infra*).

In addition to the above, in individual instances the payment, working conditions, work and leisure regime of foreign personnel employed at joint enterprises, their social security and social insurance will be regulated by Soviet legislation, 'unless otherwise stipulated by an inter-state or inter-governmental treaty to which the USSR is a party' (para. 57 of Decree 48). The provisions of international tax treaties to which the USSR is a party also apply to the taxation of joint enterprises (para. 41 of Decree 49).

The chapters in this publication represent an attempt, on the basis of early legislative acts and the first stages in their practical application, to analyze key legal problems arising from the establishment and operation of joint enterprises. In the course of further development of legislation a tendency to streamline legislative regulation has taken shape and can be expected to continue.

Legislation on joint enterprises is likely to be a subject of constant streamlining in accordance with current practices. (*Editor's note.* In this respect, readers should note the adoption of new forms of business entities, including joint stock societies.) The role of the partners in a JE in deciding vital issues on the establishment and activities of joint enterprises is thus enhanced. For example, the original legislation placed certain limits on the partners' capital shares, but later (December 1988) the issue of share distribution was left to the partners' sole discretion. It was further established that transfers of shares, risk insurance and auditing of financial and economic activities would be exercised on mutual agreement between the parties. These and similar changes are entirely consistent with the general spirit of perestroika and democratization of economic activities in the USSR as these policies have developed subsequent to their inception.

Special conditions have been created in the USSR to stimulate joint enterprises in its Far Eastern economic region, in specified areas and special economic zones (for example, favourable tax provisions and other privileges). (*Editor's note*. Laws on 'free economic zones' have been created with respect to Nakhodka, Sakhalin, St Petersburg and other territories.)

In terms of scientific systematization of a joint enterprise as a legal institution, reference should first be made to the field of international private law, due to the so-called 'foreign element' in the corresponding relationships (existence of a foreign partner, mixed capital stock, economic activity outside the country of foundation and location, etc.).

Previously Soviet legal literature dealt with general problems pertaining to various organizational forms of joint activity, mixed companies, joint enterprises and, primarily, international economic organizations of the CMEA member countries.[7] Legal matters of joint enterprises operating in the USSR were studied only in historical terms,[8] which was quite natural since joint enterprises were non-existent on the territory of the USSR in the post-war period.

The present study deals exclusively with joint enterprises established and operating on the territory of the USSR. It represents one of the first pieces of Soviet research into the new legislation. Consequently it reflects a current quest for solutions to a number of problems, aimed at streamlining the economic and legal terms most conducive to an efficient application in the USSR of this new form of international economic, scientific and technical cooperation.

NOTES

[1] Resolution 991 of the CC of the CPSU and the USSR Council of Ministers of 19 August 1986, 'On measures to improve management of foreign economic contacts'; and Resolution 992, 'On measures to improve management of economic, scientific and technological cooperation with socialist countries' (*Sobraniye postanovleniy SSSR*, Art. 172, No. 33, 1986); Resolution 1074 of 17 September 1987, 'On additional measures to improve the country's external economic activity in the new conditions of economic management' (*Ekonomicheskaya gazeta*, No. 41, 1987, pp.

18–19) and Resolution 1405 of the USSR Council of Ministers of December 1988, 'On further development of foreign economic activity of state, cooperative and other social enterprises, associations and organizations' (*Ekonomicheskaya gazeta*, No. 51, 1988, pp. 17–18).

2 N. N. Voznesenskaya, *Joint Enterprises as a Form of International Economic Cooperation*, (Moscow, 1986), p. 8 (in Russian); N. V. Mironov, 'The legal status of joint economic organizations of the CMEA member countries in the territory of the USSR', (*Sovetskoye gosudarstvo i pravo*, No. 3, 1984, p. 46); *Legal Forms of Organizing Joint Enterprises of CMEA Member Countries*, (Moscow, 1985), p. 69 (in Russian); N. N. Voznesenskaya, 'Joint enterprises with the participation of capitalist and developing countries in the territory of the USSR', (*Sovetskoye gosudarstvo i pravo*, No. 1, pp. 117–25).

3 *Legal Forms of Organizing Joint Enterprises of CMEA Member Countries*, p. 69.

4 *Vedomosti Verkhovnogo Soveta SSSR*, Art. 35, No. 2, 1987.

5 Some changes were subsequently introduced to Decree 48. See Resolution 718 of the USSR Council of Ministers of 27 June 1987, which specified and revised para. 19 of Decree 48 (*Sobraniye postanovleniy SSSR*, Art. 129, No. 40, 1987); Resolution 782 of the USSR Council of Ministers of 14 July 1987, which revised para. 57 of Decree 48 (*Sobraniye postanovleniy SSSR*, Art. 38, No. 8, 1988).

6 *Sobraniye postanovleniy SSSR*, Art. 40, No. 9, 1987. As with Decree 48, this decree was considerably amended by Resolution 352 of the USSR Council of Ministers of 17 March 1988 and Resolution 1405 of December 1988 (see Appendix 1).

7 N. N. Voznesenskaya, 'Legal forms of joint enterprise and Soviet practice', (*Sovetskoye gosudarstvo i pravo*, No 3, 1985, pp. 59–66); *idem, Joint Enterprises as a Form of International Economic Cooperation; Legal Forms of Scientific, Technical, Production and Economic Cooperation of the USSR with Foreign Firms* (Moscow, 1980), in Russian; *Legal Forms of Organizing Joint Enterprises of CMEA Member Countries*.

8 See *Legal Forms of Scientific, Technical, Production and Economic Cooperation of the USSR with Capitalist Countries* (Moscow, 1980); *Joint Enterprises, International Amalgamations and Organizations in the Territory of the USSR*, ed. by G. Golubov (Moscow, 1988), both in Russian.

1991 SUPPLEMENTARY COMMENTARY

By mid-1991 more than 3,000 joint enterprises had been registered in the USSR. In 1990 the number had doubled from what it had been in 1989, and it continues to grow. But more significant than the number of JEs is the fact that during the conditions of transition of the Soviet Union toward a market economy, JEs ceased to be the sole form of foreign investment in the country's economy. Wholly foreign-owned subsidiaries may now be created in the USSR. They may acquire property, shares, commercial paper and rights to use land and other natural resources, and they may conclude concession contracts. On conditions established under Soviet legislation, they may participate in destatization and privatization of all-Union, republic and municipal enterprises. Joint enterprises may now also be created by way of acquiring shares in existing joint stock societies.

All of these forms, and the attraction of foreign investment to the country, have been ensured by the adoption in the USSR of laws on entrepreneurial activities of individual citizens, laws on ownership, Fundamental Principles of Civil Legislation of 1991 and other Union and republic legislation. The Law on the General Principles of Entrepreneurship of Citizens in the USSR was adopted on 2 April 1991. This law allows individual citizens, Soviet and foreign alike, to participate directly in joint enterprises. (The text is set forth in full in Appendix 2.)

Perhaps of greatest significance, new legislation on foreign investments, regulating participation of foreign investors in joint enterprises and other forms of investment, was also adopted in the USSR in 1991. On 5 July 1991 the USSR Supreme Soviet adopted the Fundamental Principles of Legislation on Foreign Investment in the USSR. This law determines the basic principles of regulation of foreign investments in the USSR (see Appendix 3 for full text). Special rules of foreign investment in the republics are also determined by legislative acts of these republics. Laws in this respect were adopted in the Kazakh, Kirghiz and other republics, and a law on foreign investment, in even greater detail, was adopted on 4 July 1991 by the Russian Republic.

The all-Union law's goal is to create the necessary legal basis for the activities of foreign investors in the USSR. During the course of the Supreme Soviet's consideration of the draft of this law, the leadership proceeded from two premises: (*a*) that the attraction of foreign investment to the Soviet economy must be not conjunctural, but rather a strategic course directed toward the integration of the country into the world economy; and (*b*) that it must be organically linked with the process of privatization in the USSR.

Together with the above legislation, the practice of the Soviet Union's conclusion of bilateral treaties on the encouragement and protection of investment developed further. On 29 May 1991 the USSR ratified treaties in this sphere with Finland, Belgium and Luxembourg, Great Britain, the Federal Republic of Germany, France, the Netherlands, Canada, Italy, Austria, the People's Republic of China, Spain, Switzerland, Turkey and North Korea. It is notable in this connection that under the provisions of legislation on foreign investments, in the event that rights are granted under an international treaty which differ from those granted under Union or republic foreign investment legislation, then the provisions of the treaty prevail. Thus a legal basis promoting the organization of joint enterprises was created in the Soviet Union.

The attention of reader should also be drawn to the fact that two prior normative acts which had earlier formed the basis for joint enterprises became superfluous: 1. Decree No. 48, in relation to the creation of joint enterprises with participation of parties from CMEA countries; and 2. Decree No. 49, in relation to joint enterprises with the participation of parties from capitalist and developing countries. This development arose out of the fact that not only did the CMEA cease its activities but the existence of two separate legal regimes was no longer justified.

The legislation on foreign investments envisages the allocation to foreign investors of concessions for the exploration and exploitation of natural resources. Under the law concession contracts must be concluded between foreign investors and authorized organs of the Union and republics in the procedure established by legislative acts of the Union and republics. The law proceeds from the premise that the conditions of allocation of concessions on exploitation of natural wealth must be distinguished from the conditions of engaging in other economic activities in the USSR. Concession contracts may contain conditions which differ from the provisions of legislative acts.

In marked contrast to earlier practice, under which legislation on issues concerning joint enterprises was adopted exclusively on an all-Union level, in recent years regulation became more prevalent on a republic level, to such extent that a veritable war of laws operated for some time between the Union and republics. The conclusion of a Treaty of the Union should create a further foundation for the delineation of competence between the central government and the republics and should secure a decisive role for the republics in the regulation of these issues.

Finally it should be noted that a governmental body on foreign investment was also created. In particular, its mandate is to assist foreign investors and enterprises with foreign capital participation in their activities in the USSR.

I

The Legal Status of Joint Enterprises

The joint enterprise (JE) of participants from different countries has developed in recent decades as an effective instrument in international economic relations. Joint enterprises have become most widespread and are used by nearly all countries, including the Soviet Union.

The USSR Law on the State Enterprise (Association), adopted on 30 June 1987, referred to joint enterprises as the basic form of economic relations with capitalist and developing countries alongside industrial, scientific and technical cooperation (Art. 1, para. 3).

It is worthwhile to point out several specific features of the use of this form of cooperation in the USSR. First, the joint enterprise, being a new form of international economic cooperation, must be regarded as a revived form, since it was used by the Soviet Union in its early years. Lenin strongly supported the idea of setting up mixed companies on Soviet territory and believed it acceptable to learn the Western partners' knack of managing and carrying on export and import operations. He called upon Soviet executives to study the experience of capitalists in this sphere.[1]

However, at the time the practice was not developed on a large scale for a number of reasons. It has resumed since the 1960s. According to UNCTAD data published in June 1986,[2] the number of joint enterprises with Soviet participation totalled between 120 and 145. Of these, 30 joint enterprises had been set up in developing countries (chiefly in Africa), about ten in Asia and nine in Latin America. The USSR has also cooperated with a number of European capitalist countries: Belgium (where there were 13 joint enterprises at the beginning of 1986), Britain (where the respective figure was 13), France (12), the Federal Republic of Germany (11), Italy (8) and Finland (7).

Second, it should be noted that until recently the USSR has used joint enterprises exclusively abroad, outside Soviet territory. Third, joint enterprises set up abroad with Soviet participation were established only in the sphere of trade and fishing. There were no joint enterprises with Soviet participation in the sphere of industry. The last two features warrant the conclusion that the use of this form by the Soviet Union was limited in scope.

This situation has now changed. The year 1986 saw the adoption of important decisions on the improvement of Soviet economic development, particularly the setting of sights on the creation of joint enterprises on Soviet territory. On 13 January 1987 the USSR Council of Ministers approved Decrees 48 and 49 (mentioned in the Introduction above), and the Presidium of the USSR Supreme Soviet also passed a relevant edict. Decree 49, on joint enterprises with the participation of firms from capitalist and developing countries, sets forth the basic purposes of such joint enterprises. These include the satisfaction of the country's requirements in certain industrial products, raw materials and foodstuffs, the introduction of advanced foreign technology, managerial experience and additional material and financial resources into the national economy, and the development of the country's export facilities together with the reduction of irrational imports (para. 3). The decree thus provides not only for the creation of joint enterprises in the USSR with the participation of foreign capital, but also for the use of advantages inherent in this form of cooperation, above all in the sphere of advanced technology, know-how and managerial experience.

Decree 49 does not pinpoint the exact economic spheres in which joint enterprises may be established, nor does it strictly limit JEs as to the spheres in which they may operate. This tendency also extends to joint enterprises set up abroad with Soviet participation. Thus the aforementioned factors are responsible for the removal of restrictions in this field, which fact, no doubt, will contribute to the effective development of this promising form of international cooperation.

What is a joint enterprise? Decree 49 does not contain a definition of JEs, but an analysis of its content enables us to draw the conclusion that concepts in this sphere available in Soviet legal and economic literature may be extended to the JEs to be set up in Soviet territory. The JE may be seen in three ways: (*a*) as a form of international economic cooperation; (*b*) as a form of involving foreign investment; and (*c*) as a form of organizing pertinent economic activity. The JE is a more complex but more effective form of cooperation that implies deeper and closer ties between participants. The Soviet understanding of the JE corresponds, by and large, to the conception which has wide currency in other countries. Therefore, we can speak about joint enterprises in their basic features as a single form of international economic cooperation.

The essence of this cooperation lies in the unification of capital belonging to enterprises from different countries (in our case countries with different socio-economic systems) in joint financing and management for the purpose of achieving definite economic results, in joint taking of risks and sustaining of losses and in the distribution of profits pro rata to participation in capital. These essential features, being reflected in law in the JE's legal status, create the legal complex which distinguishes the JE from all other forms of international economic cooperation regardless of the JE's particular economic activity.

Decree 49 provides important legal principles for JEs' organization and functioning in the Soviet economy. This legislative act provides, first, for the granting of permission to set up a joint enterprise; second, for the principle of application of national (that is, Soviet) law to the JEs; and third, for the principle of contractual, not legislative, regulation of cooperation in the form of JEs.

Of special importance in defining the legal status of JEs is the second principle – the application of national legislation. It must be said that this principle is widespread in other countries and follows from the principle of state sovereignty, according to which national law operates on the whole in the territory of a sovereign state.

Paragraph 1 of Decree 49 points out the specific legislative acts applicable to JEs. These include the Edict of the Presidium of the USSR Supreme Soviet of 13 January 1987, the present decree itself, as well as certain other legislative acts of the USSR and the Union republics which include rules pertaining to juridical persons (for example, Articles 11–13 of the Fundamentals of Civil Legislation of 1961), since joint enterprises 'shall be juridicial persons according to Soviet legislation' (Decree 49, para. 6). Decree 49 also makes reference to the norms of Soviet legislation that regulate the possession, use and disposal of general property by JEs, to the norms on the protection of this property (para. 15), to the norms on the protection of industrial property (para. 17), to the Decree of the Presidium of the USSR Supreme Soviet dated 26 January 1981 (containing the norms on the collection of tax and non-tax arrears) and finally to labour and social legislation.

The decree attaches great importance to the *contractual* registration of cooperation in the form of JEs (this figures as the third principle). It contains (para. 1) the following formulation: '. . . Joint enterprises with the participation of Soviet organizations and firms of capitalist and developing countries . . . shall be created in the territory of the USSR on the basis of *contracts concluded with participants of such enterprises.*'

The very proviso that JEs are established on the basis of agreements is quite common and widespread. We have identified it as a principle because today the specific legal regulation of JEs is still incomplete, and many important questions, which are settled in other countries by law, are regulated in the Soviet Union by agreements.

Such are the basic legal principles of Decree 49. On the whole, it is comprehensive in nature, for it regulates both the conditions for the organization and functioning of JEs and the questions of investment, finances, taxation, labour and social relations and the like.

The fundamental proviso of the decree that defines the status of the JE under Soviet law is paragraph 6, which states: 'Joint enterprises are legal entities under Soviet law. They may, in their own name, contract, acquire proprietary and non-proprietary personal rights, undertake obligations, sue and be sued in courts of justice and in arbitration tribunals. Joint enterprises shall have independent balance sheets and operate on the basis of full cost-accounting, self-support and self-finance.'

Joint enterprises acquire the rights of legal entities from the time their constitutive instruments are registered with the USSR Ministry of Finance. An announcement of the formation of a JE is published in the press (para. 9).

Under paragraph 4 of the decree, a JE may be formed with the participation of one or more Soviet enterprises (amalgamation or other organization) which is a juridical person and one or more foreign firms (company, corporation or other organization) which is a juridical person.

Of fundamental importance for the JE is paragraph 18 of Decree 49, regarding limitation of liability. This provision states: 'A joint enterprise shall be liable for its obligations in all of its property. The Soviet state and the partners in a joint enterprise shall not be liable for its obligations, nor shall a joint enterprise be liable for the obligations of the Soviet state and of the partners in the enterprise.'

A JE is established on the basis of its constitutive instruments – an agreement and a statute (or charter). The decree does not contain legal rules concerning agreements. Paragraph 7 of the decree provides that a JE must have its statute approved by its partners and lists the clauses that must be included in the statute, namely 'the nature of the joint enterprise, the objectives of its operations, its legal address, the list of partners, the amount of the authorized fund, the shares of the partners therein, the procedure for raising the authorized fund (including foreign currency contents), the structure, composition and competence of the enterprise's management bodies, the decision-making procedure, the range of issues to be unanimously settled and the joint enterprise's liquidation procedure'. It continues: 'The statute may incorporate other provisions related to the specific character of joint enterprise's operations unless these are contrary to Soviet law.' It is worth noting that the provision enumerating which paragraphs are to be included in the statute does not establish any requirements as to such paragraphs' specific content. Thus, the parties in a JE have a free hand in drafting constitutive instruments.

Decree 49 does not rigidly regulate the process of setting up JEs. It states that the authorized fund is formed from the contributions of the participants, which may include buildings, structures, equipment and other fixed assets; the rights to use land, water and other natural resources together with buildings, structures and equipment; and other property rights, including the right to use inventions and know-how and financial assets including freely convertible currencies. The decree also contains rules governing the evaluation of the contributions made by the Soviet and foreign participants.

The decree provides for a two-level system of JE management. A JE's higher bodies are the board, elected by the participants, and the directorate, which is responsible for the day-to-day running of the JE. Initially the chairman of the board and the director-general were required to be Soviet citizens (para. 21); but this rule was subsequently changed to allow foreign citizens to serve as such. In point of fact all questions, including the procedure for decision-making and for appointing persons to managerial bodies, are settled by agreement between the parties and find reflection in constitutive instruments. Paragraph 31 of the decree states that the portion of the profit of the JE remaining after payments into the USSR state budget, and after investments have been made for the creation and replenishment of the JE's funds, is divided among the JE's participants in proportion to their shares in the authorized fund.

Decree 49 contains other important clauses related to the legal status of JEs. For example, the JEs have the right independently to conduct export and import operations. The import and export of goods by JEs are effected on the basis of licences issued in the statutory manner (para. 24).

Of great importance is paragraph 23, which to some extent determines the legal status of a JE in the Soviet economy. It says that Soviet state bodies do not issue obligatory planned assignments to the JE and that the sale of its products is not guaranteed by the Soviet state. The JE is independent in formulating and authorizing the programmes of its own economic activity. By agreement with Soviet enterprises and organizations, JEs determine the type of currency to be used in settlements for the products sold and bought, the procedure for the sale of their products on the Soviet market and the procedure for the delivery of goods from this market.

By and large, together with other pieces of Soviet legislation, Decree 49 outlines the legal status of a JE with participation of foreign capital in the Soviet territory. The existing gaps in the decree are being bridged by other legal acts. For example, the USSR Ministry of Finance adopted the instruction 'On the procedure for registering joint enterprises established on Soviet territory' (No. 224 of 24 November 1987). This instruction forbids state, cooperative and other social enterprises and economic organizations from concluding transactions with a JE prior to the latter's registration. Soviet banks may open current and settlement accounts on behalf of JEs, issue monetary resources to them and conduct credit and settlement operations with them only after they are registered in the statutory manner.

Many foreign authors have asked whether the USSR Law on the State Enterprise (Association) applies to JEs. We answer this in the negative.

An overall analysis of the legal acts regulating the organization and functioning of JEs in different countries testifies to the fact that such enterprises, being a new form of economic cooperation, do not represent a novelty from the standpoint of law, since they fit in with the traditional model of a commercial association with several (chiefly two) modifications. In other countries, joint enterprises are created for the most part in the form of a joint stock company or limited partnership.

It must be noted in this connection that all countries have elaborated legal rules on joint stock companies and limited partnerships and have made them law. Joint enterprises set up abroad with Soviet participation are also either joint stock companies or limited partnerships. Analogous Soviet laws on JEs can be expected to be drafted in the near future.

In the past the Soviet Union has had a Statute on Joint Stock Societies. The statute was adopted in 1927 but was repealed in 1962 after the Fundamentals of Civil Legislation of 1961 came into force. The absence of rules on the legal forms of JEs must be regarded as a crucial gap, since such rules, when elaborated in detail (often peremptory), assist parties to a JE to draft constitutive instruments in a proper way and also to simplify and hasten the process of founding JEs. What is more important, though, is the fact that such rules provide an effective control over the establishment and functioning of JEs. (*Editor's note.* Legislation on joint stock societies and limited responsibility societies was adopted by the USSR and the RSFSR in 1990. These and other entities are now envisaged under the Fundamental Principles of Legislation on Foreign Investment in the USSR – see Appendix 3 – as well as the new Fundamental Principles of Civil Legislation of the USSR and Republics adopted on 31 May 1991.)

When joint enterprises and other commercial and industrial companies are formed and registered abroad, special agencies carry on a detailed verification of the correspondence of the terms of their constitutive instruments to the rules of the host country's laws on joint stock companies with an eye to the legal model that has been chosen by the partners. Where founders violate such rules, they may be held liable not only materially but also criminally.

Western countries have introduced the normative method of founding enterprises (joint stock companies, corporations, etc.) without prior permission, while the USSR has adopted the authorization method. Nevertheless, it would be wrong to assume that the former countries exercise less stringent control over this process. In fact Western nations regulate all major questions involved in the process of founding companies so succinctly and in such detail that effective control is guaranteed by simply conforming with the law.

In our view priority must be given to the drafting of rules that would govern in detail and define in an orderly manner the process of founding JEs. It would be incorrect to say that this process boils down to the drafting of constitutive instruments (although this is not a simple matter) and to their registration (upon which a JE becomes a subject of law). The process of founding JEs, apart from preliminary feasibility studies of profitability and the need for setting up a particular JE, is quite complex and has several aspects, the chief ones being the legal, financial, economic and organizational aspects.

In this connection Soviet jurists suggest the need, in the legal regulation of JEs, to define in clear and concrete terms the process of their organization in every aspect: (*a*) in a purely legal aspect by compiling constitutive instruments, defining their form, duration and methods of endorsement; (*b*) in a financial aspect which defines the procedure and the term of making contributions to the authorized capital and the procedure and forms of certifying the same, and which also allows or prohibits the possibility of making payments in instalments in certain periods; and (*c*) in an organizational aspect, which presupposes the granting to institutions of complex of rights and duties and their bearing responsibility (liability). A solution must be found to the question as to the time when constitutive instruments are endorsed. In our opinion, the introduction of a definite amount of money – say, not less than a quarter of the authorized fund – is quite necessary before the concluding stage of the legalization of a JE.

Thus on the one hand Decree 49 fixes the principle of applying Soviet law to JEs, and on the other hand it would in a sufficient manner regulate the whole range of legal relations arising during the foundation of JEs on Soviet territory.

In our view this principle does not exclude the possibility of choosing a particular law. We believe that this possibility is admissible in the regulation of relations whose subjects are the JE participants, that is, a foreign firm and a Soviet organization and not the JEs themselves (their activity being regulated by Soviet legislation alone).

Soviet doctrine allows the choice of law during the conclusion of contracts with foreign partners. For example, Article 126 of the Fundamentals of Civil Legislation of 1961 states: 'The rights and duties of the parties to a foreign trade transaction shall be determined pursuant to the laws of the place where it is made, unless otherwise provided for by agreement of the parties.' Consequently the relations between a foreign firm and a Soviet organization in the formation of a JE may be regulated by mutual agreement of the parties not by Soviet but by foreign law. For example, a contract whereunder a foreign partner would deliver equipment or technology to the USSR as a contribution to the capital of a JE might be concluded under foreign law.

As for the foundation agreement under which a JE (a legal entity under Soviet law, according to Decree 49) is formed, in our opinion it should be legalized under Soviet law, although there are no particular rules for this matter. We think that until such rules are drafted it is possible to make use of some model of a foreign law in drawing up the agreement's terms. The legal status of the JE as a Soviet juridical person, however, will be determined under Soviet law. (*Editor's note.* The rule on applicable law has been clarified under the Fundamental Principles of Civil Legislation of 1991 to apply the law of the place of a joint enterprise's foundation.)

In retrospect the emphasis on the contractual and not the legislative legalization of relations in connection with JEs must be regarded as a temporary phenomenon. In this light Decree 49 should be interpreted under review as a legal document which has decided the fundamental question of the possibility to set up on Soviet territory enterprises with the participation of foreign capital. However, the decree makes it imperative to draft relevant Soviet legislation.

Legislation in this sphere must be improved above all through the elaboration of the legal status of JEs. It is advisable to make use of those legal forms which all countries of the world have adopted – the joint stock company and the limited partnership. Such legislation may be based on the law of any country from which we could borrow the technically legal form. The legal form remains a form: in different socio-economic conditions it mediates the content that corresponds to them.

NOTES

[1]   V.I. Lenin, *Complete Works*, 5th edition, Moscow, Vol. 42, pp. 79–83 (in Russian).
[2]   UNCTAD(st), zSc15, 20 June 1986, p. 18.

1991 SUPPLEMENTARY COMMENTARY

An essential step on the path of creation of joint enterprises was the restoration in Soviet legislation of the regulation of various types of economic societies and companies, mentioned in Chapter I. The legal status of individual types of such societies and companies is determined by legislative acts, for example, the Statute on Joint Stock

Societies and Societies of Limited Responsibility, confirmed by the USSR Council of Ministers on 19 June 1990, and the RSFSR Statute on Joint Stock Societies, confirmed by the RSFSR Council of Ministers on 25 December 1990.

In a society of limited responsibility, the charter fund is divided into participatory shares. The proportions of such shares are determined by the society's charter. The society's participants bear losses in connection with the society's activities within the limits of their investments.

In a joint stock society, the charter fund is divided into a definite number of stocks. Stockholders incur losses only to extent of the value of the stock they hold.

Under the 1991 Fundamental Principles of Legislation on Foreign Investment in the USSR, joint enterprises may now be created in the form of joint stock societies, societies of limited responsibility and any other forms which are not contrary to legislative acts of the USSR and the republics. Special rules apply to the acquisition of shares by foreign investors in various individual republics. For example, in the RSFSR an enterprise shall be considered to be one with foreign participation (and therefore eligible for privileges granted to such enterprises) *only* where the foreign investor either has paid for its share in foreign currency, or has acquired more than 50 per cent of the shares.

II

Joint Enterprises in the Soviet Legal System and Their Part in Economic Turnover

1. Joint Enterprises in the Soviet Legal System

A major condition for the activity of a joint enterprise on the territory of the USSR with the participation of Soviet organizations and of firms of foreign countries is the availability of the appropriate economic prerequisites. In principle such enterprises can successfully perform only in the context of production relations based on economic methods of management.

In essence a joint enterprise is a commodity producer which enters into numerous economic and other relations with various organizations, both within the country and abroad. At home this entails relations with state enterprises and organizations, governmental and administrative bodies and agencies; outside the country it entails relations in the world economic market and relations of foreign partners of joint enterprises with their own parent companies and shareholders.

This is not the first time in the history of the Soviet state when the question has arisen regarding activities in Soviet territory of joint enterprises with participation of foreign capital. Such enterprises were first set up in the early 1920s during the introduction of the New Economic Policy (NEP), the period of revival and development of commodity-money relations in the Soviet economy.

According to the resolution of the Presidium of the All-Russia Central Executive Committee on Foreign Trade of 13 March 1922, the People's Commissariat for Foreign Trade was entitled, with the approval of the Council for Labour and Defence (CLD), to set up joint stock companies ('Russian, foreign and joint') with a view to realizing export–import transactions and producing export-oriented commodities. In the case of joint stock companies the Soviet side was to hold no less than 51 per cent of the stock capital. By 1 January 1925 there were 52 joint stock companies in the USSR, including 12 with foreign participation. In January 1926 the Russian-American company for producing compressed gas (RAGAS) was founded, and it operated until 1931.

Special legislation on trading partnerships regulated the activities of joint stock companies with the participation of foreign capital. The section of the Civil Code of the RSFSR of 1922 entitled Law of Obligations, dealt with various types of companies, such as partnerships, unlimited companies, limited partnerships, companies limited by guarantee and joint stock companies. Similar sections were included in the civil codes of the other Union republics. On 27 August 1927 the Central Executive Committee and the Council of People's Commissars of the USSR passed the All-Union Statute on Joint Stock Companies.

In the early 1930s, however, the overwhelming majority of joint stock companies on the territory of the USSR ceased to exist.

In 1986, for the second time, the question was raised regarding joint enterprises with the participation of Soviet organizations and of firms of capitalist and developing countries. In accordance with the decisions of the 27th Congress of the CPSU on national economic management, the USSR began the transition to economic methods of management. Soviet enterprises and production associations began the transfer to a system of full cost-accounting, based on self-support and self-financing. The system of state planning started to become more flexible and comprehensive. Extensive development of commodity–money relations also started.

The provisions of the Law of the USSR on the State Enterprise (Association) were backed up by Decree 49 of the USSR Council of Ministers, paragraph 6 of which states: 'Joint enterprises shall have an independent balance sheet and operate on the basis of full economic accountability, non-subsidy and self-financing.'

The inclusion of joint enterprises in the system of production relations in 1987 was aimed at a fuller satisfaction of needs in specific types of industrial products, raw materials and foodstuffs, the attraction to the Soviet national economy of progressive foreign technology and equipment, management experience, additional material and financial resources, the development of the country's export base and the reduction of its irrational imports (Decree 49, para 3).

Joint enterprises with the participation of firms of foreign countries cannot be referred to as state enterprises. However, with respect to their legal status, joint enterprises operating in the Soviet Union are the result of legal relationships formed in accordance with, and coming under the full jurisdiction of, the law of the Soviet Union.

Until the adoption in 1986 of special normative acts on joint enterprises, previous Soviet legislation did not incorporate the legal rules regulating the formation and operation of joint enterprises in the territory of the USSR, with the exception of the Edict of the Presidium of the USSR Supreme Soviet of 1983 'On the procedure for the activity of joint economic organizations of the USSR and other CMEA member countries on the territory of the USSR'. However, this instrument did not cover joint enterprises between Soviet organizations and firms of capitalist and developing countries.

To what extent were the normative acts of 1987 consistent with the general system of Soviet legislation?

First, we should examine whether such acts were in accord with the USSR constitution. Neither the 1977 constitution nor the constitutions of the Union or autonomous republics mention the establishment of joint enterprises with the participation of foreign firms on the territory of the USSR.

Chapter 2 of the USSR constitution, on the economic system, merely recites the socialist ownership of the means of production and details the private property of Soviet citizens. Article 16 of the constitution defines the economic structure of the USSR and principles of management of its national economy but does not expressly envisage joint enterprises. Finally, Article 37 guarantees the rights and liberties accorded to foreign citizens and stateless persons under Soviet laws but makes no reference at all to enterprises or other types of juridical persons.

However, at the same time, the USSR constitution contains no bans on the establishment and operation of joint enterprises on the territory of the USSR. The constitution is based on the principle according to which any activity is allowed in the Soviet Union if it is lawful and is not detrimental to the interests of society and the state or to the rights and legitimate interests of Soviet citizens.

The above permits a general conclusion to be drawn: the establishment in the territory of the USSR and operation of joint enterprises between Soviet and foreign organizations do not contradict the spirit or letter of the USSR constitution. Moreover, the possibility of joint enterprises in the territory of the USSR indirectly ensues from Article 29 of the constitution, which among other principles of USSR foreign policy specifies the principle of cooperation between states. Such conclusion is corroborated by Decree 49 which underlines that it has been adopted 'with a view to the further development of trade, economic, scientific and technical cooperation with capitalist and developing countries on a stable and mutually advantageous basis'.

At the time Decree 49 was adopted no branches of Soviet law, including civil legislation, incorporated legal rules for joint enterprises to be established in the territory of the USSR. In the preparation of the Fundamentals of Civil Legislation of 1961 and the civil codes of the Union republics, provisions for trading partnerships were merely omitted, though they had been recorded in previously enacted legislation. (*Editor's note.* The Fundamental Principles of Civil Legislation of 1991, as well as other recent legislation, now set forth rules applicable to joint enterprises; see, for example, Appendices 2 and 3.)

But in contrast to the USSR constitution, the other normative acts mentioned above included certain provisions which could regulate the activities of joint enterprises under consideration. For example, Article 2 of the Fundamentals of Civil Legislation of 1961, which defined the range of relations regulated by civil laws, included relationships with the participation of other organizations in cases covered by the USSR legislation. In our opinion, such organizations could embrace joint enterprises. Article 11 of the Fundamentals of Civil Legislation of 1961 on juridical persons, in addition to state, collective farm and other cooperative organizations and their associations, other public organizations and their enterprises and agencies, state farms and other state cooperative organizations, admitted the legitimacy of other organizations where provided by USSR legislation.

The legal rules specified in the normative acts of 1987 on joint enterprises represent for the most part special legal rules. Joint enterprises in their activities are guided by the legislative acts of the USSR and the Union republics, with exemptions stipulated in international agreements of the USSR. (Such agreements may, for example, be signed to avoid double taxation of income due foreign participants in joint enterprises when transferring it abroad.)

As is known, special legal rules have priority over general legal rules. Any reference to the latter is permitted only in the absence of special legal rules. Nonetheless, in some cases the legislator directly cites general legal rules. For example, paragraph 48 of Decree 49 stipulates that the work and leisure regime of Soviet citizens working at joint enterprises, and their social security and insurance, shall be regulated by norms of Soviet legislation.

On the whole, special legal rules in the field under consideration regulate mainly the relationships arising from the establishment of joint enterprises, organization of their inner structure and management, taxation and certain specific aspects of their activities which bear on the interests of society and the state. On the other hand, economic relationships of joint enterprises with other enterprises, associations and organizations as a rule come under general legislation.

In economic terms a joint enterprise represents a single complex of material, non-material and manpower factors of production. In legal terms it operates as an enterprise (not an organization), such as a trading partnership, which is recognized as a juridical person under Soviet law. In legal terms, an enterprise is regarded as a *subject* of law, not as an *object* of law. This directly ensues from Article 11 of the USSR constitution of 1977. While enumerating the objects of state property, Article 11 lists 'the property of state-run trade organizations and public utilities and other state-run undertakings', not the enterprises themselves, as was previously the case in the USSR constitution of 1936.

The Soviet Union has applied the concept of a juridical person in relation to enterprises. Western countries, with the exception of Liechtenstein, do not adhere to this principle. In such countries, public companies act as juridical persons, while the enterprises which belong to such companies are viewed as the objects of law.

The Soviet concept of a juridical person is also applicable to joint enterprises established and operating in the territory of the USSR. The normative acts of 1987 deal explicitly with enterprises, but not with trading partnerships. Therefore, in strict legal terms, these acts do not cover the cases of joint stock companies or other types of trading partnerships whose establishment in the territory of the USSR may be necessitated. The Fundamentals of Civil Legislation of 1961 contain no bans on the organization of such juridical persons, but their organization would require the adoption of a special law. It would be expedient to adopt an independent normative act in this connection. (*Editor's note*. In 1990 the USSR and the RSFSR both adopted normative acts on joint stock societies.)

Furthermore, according to Article 12 of the Fundamentals of Civil Legislation of 1961 and the corresponding articles in the civil codes of the Union republics, a juridical person possesses civil legal capacity in conformity with the specified objectives of its activity. In other words it may exercise its activity on the basis of the principle of special franchise. This provision, however, cannot be understood as limiting. As is noted in the commentary to Article 26 of the RSFSR Civil Code, the statute can hardly provide an exhaustive listing of transactions to be concluded for the objectives of a juridical person. Even the most detailed list might be incomplete, which could hamper the activity of a juridical person and make its goals unattainable. Therefore it should be acknowledged that a juridical person may enter into any legal relationships which agree with the objectives specified in its statute, including those legal relationships which indirectly contribute to realization of such objectives. Arbitration procedures are also based on this principle.

Further support for a broad-minded approach to the concept of special franchise of a juridical person is the provision of Article 1 in the Law on the State Enterprise (Association), which elucidates the notion of enterprise.

The above propositions are fully applicable to joint enterprises as well. Paragraph 7 of Decree 49 states: 'The charter shall determine the object and purposes of the activities of the enterprise . . .' With a view to realizing these objectives, as may be seen from the decree's subsequent provisions, joint enterprises are entitled to conclude any transactions and undertake any actions envisaged by law, including export and import transactions in the world market.

It goes without saying that a JE bears independent legal responsibility for unlawful actions. Paragraph 18 of Decree 49 endorses the principle of separate property liability of a JE on its obligations, with the JE being liable in all of its property, including the fixed assets. This principle lies in strict contrast to the liability of Soviet state organizations: under Article 2 of the Fundamentals of Civil Legislation of 1961, garnishment as regards buildings, structures, equipment and other property making up the fixed assets of state organizations cannot be levied to satisfy creditors' claims. (The same limitations also apply to the property of collective farms, other cooperative organizations and their associations, trade union and other public organizations.)

Lastly, the final provision on the status of joint enterprises in the general system of civil law – the legal nature of the rights of a joint enterprise to the property under its charge – should be noted. It is known that in relation to the property of Soviet cooperative and public organizations the regime of the right of *ownership* is applied; as regards the property of state enterprises, associations and organizations, their treatment is based on the right of *operative management*. The property rights of joint enterprises are still not clear under the law. Paragraph 15 of Decree 49 states: 'A joint enterprise shall exercise, in accordance with Soviet legislation, the possession, use and disposition of its property in accordance with the purpose of its activities and purpose of its property.' But the law says nothing of the legal basis of this right, calling for a more precise elaboration of its legal nature.

In our view, the rights of joint enterprises to their property should be rights of *ownership*. As for the objects which make up the exclusive ownership of the state (land, forests, minerals, water), rights thereto may also be considered, as mentioned above, part of the charter fund of a joint enterprise. Furthermore, a joint enterprise may lease property, including land.

2. *Legal Forms of Participation of Joint Enterprises in the Economic Turnover*

Soviet legislation on joint enterprises contains three principal groups of legal rules regulating the participation of such enterprises in the economic turnover. The first group is comprised of the rules which specify the most general and fundamental issues arising from such participation. They make up the basis of the other two groups, one of which deals with the legal forms of participation of joint enterprises in the external economic turnover and the other with legal forms of participation in the internal economic turnover.

The first premise for participation of joint enterprises in the economic turnover is to empower them with the legal capacity of a juridical person (Decree 49, para. 6).

The concept of a juridical person is one of the fundamental categories in Soviet civil law. Recognition of joint enterprises as juridical persons in many respects establishes the basis for their participation in the economic turnover. By virtue of such recognition, joint enterprises are entitled to enter into agreements on their own behalf, acquire property and personal rights, bear obligations and act as plaintiffs and defendants in courts and arbitration tribunals.

The recognition of joint enterprises as juridical persons is a notable step in the development of Soviet civil law, motivated by the fact that only organizations belonging to the type specified in the law can be treated as juridical persons. Until recently such listing included state organizations and agencies (meeting certain requirements), collective farms, inter-farm and other cooperative and public organizations and their associations, as well as state farm and other state cooperative organizations (Art. 11 of the Fundamental Principles of Civil Legislation of 1961). Such organizations in all of their parameters were purely Soviet phenomena. Now enterprises with the participation of companies from foreign countries are also recognized as juridical persons.

Soviet legal literature identifies four characteristic features of a juridical person. The first is its *organizational integrity*, expressed in a well-established structural form, namely the existence of a conventional order of relationships between parties within the organization. Organizational integrity is endorsed by a document which may be typical or individual. Decree 49, for example, envisages that a joint enterprise should have a charter to be approved by its members. The charter, among other things, should define the number of its members, the structure, composition and powers of managerial bodies, the procedure of decision-making and the range of matters requiring unanimous decision (para. 7). The charter may incorporate other provisions specific to the activities in which the joint enterprise is engaged.

The second feature of a juridical person is its *possession of its own property*. As applied to a joint enterprise, this is manifest in the fact that its property is separate from the property of its parties, and from the property of other organizations or citizens. Under Decree 49 the property of a joint enterprise should comprise the charter fund and reserve funds (paragraphs 10, 30). Other funds necessary for its activity and social development may also be established as provided in its foundation documents.

The existence of the charter fund is the most characteristic feature of separation of property of a JE. This fund, comprised of the shares of its parties, may be replenished by the income from the JE's economic activity and by additional contributions of its parties. Decree 49 envisages that the charter fund may be made up of contributions in the form of buildings, structures, equipment, the right to use land, water, other natural resources, buildings, structures and equipment and also other property rights (including rights to use inventions and know-how) and cash in freely convertible currency or in the currency of the countries of the parties to the JE (para. 11).

The third feature of a juridical person is its *independent property liability*. As a juridical person a JE is liable for its obligations in all of its property (para. 18). Decree 49 expressly states that the JE is not liable for the obligations of its parties, that is Soviet enterprises (associations and other organizations) or Western corporations, companies or other firms. In turn, Soviet and foreign parties bear no responsibility for the obligations of the joint enterprise (para. 18).

Of major importance is the special provision that the Soviet state is not responsible for a JE's obligations and that the JE bears no responsibility for the obligations of the Soviet state. This rule ensues from the provision that the Soviet side in a JE can be represented only by those enterprises (associations and other organizations) which are themselves juridical persons (para. 4). In this capacity such enterprises are also independent in their liability for their obligations. The law provides explicitly: 'The state shall not be liable for the obligations of state organizations which are juridical persons while these organizations shall not be liable for the obligations of the state' (Art. 13, part 2 of the Fundamental Principles of 1961).

Thus where a Soviet state enterprise is a party to a joint enterprise, the liability of the latter for its obligations is separate from the liability of the Soviet state both by virtue of para. 4 of Decree 49 and Article 13 of the Fundamental Principles of 1961.

The independent liability of a joint enterprise is, however, distinct as compared with the independent liability of other juridical persons (except for cooperatives): it is unlimited. Other juridical persons are liable only in that property the execution upon which may be levied according to the legislation of the USSR and the Union republics (Art. 13, part 1 of the Fundamental Principles of 1961). Decree 49 states: 'A joint enterprise shall be liable for its obligations with all the property which belongs to it' (para. 18, part 1). For the sake of comparison, we note that according to the civil code of the RSFSR, garnishment cannot be levied to satisfy a creditor's claims as regards enterprises, buildings, structures, equipment and other property making up the fixed assets of state organizations (Art. 98). (*Editor's note*. USSR and RSFSR legislation no longer contains this distinction.)

Decree 49 incorporates a legal rule which is in fact an obvious aftermath of its other rules, and quite justifiable in view of the novelty of the problem: execution upon the property of a joint enterprise can be levied only by the decision of bodies which are entitled, under Soviet legislation, to examine disputes involving joint enterprises (para. 15, part 2). As we shall see below, the matter may be considered by either the Soviet courts or arbitration tribunals.

Finally, the fourth feature of a juridical person is that it *acts on its own behalf* in the economic turnover. Envisaging that joint enterprises sign agreements, acquire rights, bear obligations and act as plaintiff and defendant, the decree specifies that they do so 'in their own name' (para. 6).

The second premise for participation of a joint enterprise in the economic turnover is of a legal–property nature. Decree 49 contains rules specifying the rights of an enterprise to its property. The decree endorses a joint enterprise's right under Soviet legislation to exercise 'the possession, use and disposition of its property in accordance with the purpose of its activities and purpose of the property' (para. 15, part 1).

The above-mentioned formula of possession, use and disposal is widely applied in Soviet civil law, primarily to enforce the independence of a party to a civil legal relationship from other parties involved in the economic turnover in matters concerning the treatment of such party's property. This formula is traditional; indeed, Soviet civil law has applied it since the early 1920s. Soviet civil law now in force employs this formula also to specify the status of the owner of specific property. According to the Fundamentals, 'an owner is entitled to possess, use and dispose of its property within the terms stipulated by law' (Art. 19).

The enforcement of independence of a joint enterprise in matters concerned with the treatment of its property by means of the formula traditionally employed in Soviet jurisprudence establishes a stable legal basis for joint enterprises.

The independence of a joint enterprise from the other parties in the economic turnover in respect of its property does not mean, of course, its independence from law. The decree establishes that its possession, use and disposal of the property are determined, above all, by the purposes of its activity. At the same time, the possession, use and disposal of the property should be in conformity with the purpose of the property. The use of property which is contradictory to its purpose (for example its destruction in the absence of economic necessity) constitutes an infringement of the law. Soviet law has never recognized the owner's right to abuse his property. This right was once acknowledged in Roman law, but a trend against this can easily be traced in the modern legislation of various countries.

Finally, the third premise for participation of joint enterprises in the economic turnover lies in the provisions which define the principles of legal protection of their rights. In this field, likewise in the majority of other cases, legislation proceeds from the general notion of *equity*, with joint enterprises being equated with the privileged right-holders in Soviet civil law, namely, state organizations. Decree 49 states: 'The property rights of a joint enterprise shall be subject to being protected in accordance with the provision of Soviet legislation established for Soviet state organizations' (para. 15, part 2).

Soviet law provides a higher level of protection for state property than for the other forms of property existing in the USSR, most importantly in civil law protection.

For example, in the sphere of civil law, an owner is entitled to initiate an action for recovery of his property from another person's unlawful possession (Art. 28, part 1 of the 1961 Fundamentals). An exception is provided from this general rule: where property is acquired for value from a person who did not have the right to alienate it, which fact the acquirer did not know and should not have known (that is, a bona fide purchaser), then the owner has the right to recover such property from the acquirer *only* when the property has been lost by the owner or person to whom the property was transferred in possession by the owner, has been stolen from one of them or has otherwise left their possession against their will (Art. 28, part 2 of the 1961 Fundamentals).

This exception does not apply to the property of a state enterprise. The 1961 Fundamentals stipulate that 'state property unlawfully alienated by any means shall be recovered by the appropriate organizations from any grantee' (Art. 28, part 4). Since a joint enterprise in the matters of legal protection is equated with Soviet state organizations, it is entitled to recover its property from any transferee, including a bona fide purchaser.

A similar provision exists also in the matter of legal protection of property rights in Soviet criminal law. The Criminal Code of the RSFSR, for example, provides for a much graver punishment for the theft of state property than for the theft of personal property (Arts. 89 and 144). Correspondingly, theft of a joint enterprise's property should be prosecuted in the same manner as theft of state property.

Finally, it should be noted that Decree 49 provides for the immunity of a joint enterprise's property against requisition or administrative confiscation (para. 15, part 1). (*Editor's note.* This rule was considerably strengthened under the provisions of the Fundamental Principles of Legislation on Foreign Investments in the USSR; see Appendix 3.)

External Economic Turnover. International economic turnover is a major sphere of the activities of a joint enterprise because its currency expenditures, including payment of income and other sums due to the foreign parties to the enterprise, must be secured first of all by the realization of its products in the foreign market. Decree 49 provides certain legal prerequisites intended to allow a JE to meet this requirement. For example, a JE may independently effect export and import transactions necessary for its economic activity (para. 24, part 1). This gives rise to an extensive range of civil law problems.

The first matter to be solved is the question of the 'national origins' of a joint enterprise whose inherent characteristics link it both with the USSR and with one or several other countries. This situation, well known to the legislators of the majority of foreign states, arises in Soviet civil law for the first time. Until now, Soviet legal doctrine was based on the firm belief that such questions were of purely theoretical interest since the composition of juridical persons existing in the USSR did not link them in any way to another country – the juridical persons which formerly represented the Soviet side in the external economic turnover were in all parameters exclusively Soviet.

At present the situation has changed, and the issue of the 'nationality' of a joint enterprise is still pending. In our opinion, in addressing this issue we must first proceed from the fact that, under Decree 49, a joint enterprise is a juridical person under Soviet legislation (para. 6). This circumstance underscores that a joint enterprise which is established in the USSR should be regarded as having Soviet 'nationality'. However, this circumstance has multifarious implications, since Soviet civil legislation regulating the external economic turnover contains a great number of rules pertaining to Soviet organizations.

The first implication does not so much concern joint enterprises themselves as those foreign firms which are their potential partners. The 1961 Fundamentals prescribe that foreign enterprises and organizations can without any special clearance effect foreign-trade transactions in the USSR and the ensuing accounting, insurance and other transactions with Soviet foreign-trade associations and other Soviet organizations entitled to effect such transactions (Art. 124). Since a joint enterprise is of Soviet 'nationality', it should be treated as one of 'the other Soviet organizations' entitled to sign foreign-trade transactions. Therefore, any foreign enterprises and organizations can freely sign agreements with a joint enterprise established in the USSR.

Accordingly, a joint enterprise is free in its choice of partners in export and import transactions and the ensuing accounting, insurance and other transactions. There is one exception from this rule: Decree 49 establishes the administrative procedure for obtaining credits by a joint enterprise in foreign banks and firms (para. 27). Therefore, if a joint enterprise is to deal with a foreign bank or firm (including those with representations in the USSR) with a view to obtaining credits, it must obtain the approval of the USSR Bank for Foreign Economic Affairs (Vnesheconombank).

Recognition of Soviet 'nationality' of a joint enterprise implies that its agreements and other transactions with foreign enterprises and organizations should come under Soviet legislation on foreign-trade transactions.

The Soviet legal doctrine regards as foreign-trade transactions those transactions in which at least one of the parties is a foreign natural or legal person and where the matter concerns import or export of commodities or any auxiliary transactions related thereto. Transactions effected by a joint enterprise in external economic turnover meet this definition.

Consequently, a number of legal issues arise. The first pertains to the form of transactions. The Soviet legal doctrine proceeds from the premise that in principle the form of a transaction is determined by the place of contract (*locus contractus*). However, the form of a transaction effected by a Soviet organization in the external economic turnover is regarded as one of the issues incorporated in the charter of such organization and, therefore, is subject to its private laws. Since a joint enterprise is of Soviet 'nationality', it is governed by the following legal rule:

The form of foreign-trade transactions made by Soviet organizations and the procedure for their signing, irrespective of the place of contract, shall be determined by USSR legislation (Art. 125, part 1 of the 1961 Fundamentals).

The decree of the USSR Council of Ministers of 14 February 1978, 'On the procedure for signing foreign-trade transactions',[1] ruled that such contracts must be effected *in writing*. Furthermore, a certain procedure for their signing was also prescribed, under which such contracts must be signed by *two persons*.

The content of an agreement between a joint enterprise and a foreign partner is naturally determined by the parties concerned. However, the mode of payment agreed upon in the contract must correspond to Soviet currency laws according to which all remittances from abroad (and vice versa) must be effected through Soviet banks, primarily through Vnesheconombank. Decree 49 stipulates that a joint enterprise must keep its foreign currency with Vnesheconombank. This currency must be spent for the purposes connected with its activities (para. 29, part 1). (*Editor's note*. Under new rules adopted by the USSR State Bank – Gosbank – in 1991, joint enterprises may now maintain accounts with any bank empowered by Gosbank.)

The basic juridical issue of the participation of a joint enterprise in external economic turnover is the law applicable to transactions entered into with foreign partners.

Here Soviet legislation is based on the principle of *volitional autonomy* (Art. 126, part 1 of the 1961 Fundamentals), which is familiar to many foreign legal systems and has gained wide recognition over the last decade. Under Soviet law the parties are free to enter into an agreement stipulating by which country's law their foreign-trade transactions shall be governed. They may choose any legal system irrespective of whether the transaction at hand has any nexus with such a system. Such law should, of course, be some national law. The sides should not subject the transaction to the rules operating beyond the national legal systems existing in the present-day world (for instance, the rules of fairness). All of this makes for a flexible solution of the problem, which may acquire a decisive importance in the case of certain disputes.

In the absence of an agreement on the choice of governing law for a transaction made by a joint enterprise in external economic turnover (as in the case of a foreign-trade transaction), the 1961 Fundamentals prescribe the following rule:

The rights and obligations of the parties in a foreign-trade transaction shall be determined by its *locus contractus* (Art. 126, part 1).

If a difficulty arises in deciding in which place the transaction has been made, it is settled by the rule stipulated in the 1961 Fundamentals to the effect that the place of a contract shall be determined by Soviet law (Art. 126, part 2).

Of considerable importance in external economic turnover is the issue of settlement of disputes. Decree 49 envisages two methods of settling disputes arising between a joint enterprise and its foreign partner (para. 20). The first method is an arbitration tribunal, the appeal to which requires the consent of the parties to the dispute. According to the RSFSR Code of Civil Procedure:

> In cases stipulated by law or international agreements a dispute arising in civil legal relationships may be referred for consideration, if the parties have agreed upon it, to the arbitration tribunal, the Maritime Arbitration Commission or the Arbitration Tribunal (Art. 27).

The sides are free in their choice of the place of arbitration. A joint enterprise, upon agreement with its foreign partner, may therefore choose arbitration in the Soviet Union. In this case it is entitled to transfer the dispute for consideration to standing Soviet arbitration organizations or an arbitration commission which is expressly set up for settling a particular type of dispute.

In the USSR disputes arising from foreign-trade transactions are referred for consideration to the Arbitration Tribunal, while disputes related to maritime law are referred to the Maritime Arbitration Commission. Both operate under the USSR Chamber of Commerce and Industry and are non-governmental organizations.

Under Soviet law an agreement by the parties to refer a dispute for resolution by an arbitration commission is binding. For example, the RSFSR Code of Civil Procedure requires a judge to dismiss a complaint 'if the parties have previously agreed upon transferring the given dispute for consideration by an arbitration tribunal' (Art. 129, para. 6).

The second method of settling disputes between a joint enterprise and its foreign partner is to bring an action in court. As mentioned earlier, as a juridical person a joint enterprise may act as a plaintiff and defendant in court. Where the parties to a foreign-trade transaction have not signed an agreement to transfer a dispute for resolution by an arbitration tribunal, disputes involving a joint enterprise are subject to the jurisdiction of Soviet courts. The status of foreign partners of a joint enterprise in civil procedure is determined by the rule of the

Fundamentals of Civil Judicial Proceedings of the USSR and the Union Republics, according to which 'foreign enterprises and organizations are entitled to bring an action in the Soviet courts and enjoy the civil procedural rights for protecting their interests' (Art. 29, part 2). Where a foreign partner brings suit against a joint enterprise in the Soviet court, the general rules for the venue of civil cases would apply. For example, the RSFSR Code of Civil Procedure requires that a suit against a juridical person be brought in the locality of the agency or the property of such person (Art. 117).

Decree 49 envisages not only the JE's right to independent participation in the external economic turnover, but also the manner in which it may exercise such right: a JE may effect export and import transactions either through Soviet foreign-trade organizations or through the marketing network of foreign parties (para. 24, part 2). The decree stipulates that such transactions are made in accordance with the respective agreements.

From a legal perspective such agreements vary in their nature. For example, when a joint enterprise signs an agreement on export or import of commodities with a foreign organization or enterprise which is part of the marketing network of a foreign party to a joint enterprise, this agreement is deemed a *foreign-trade transaction*, and all of the above requirements pertaining to foreign-trade transactions apply to it (such as that it be set in writing, that it meet the two-signature requirement, etc.).

However, an agreement between a joint enterprise and a Soviet foreign-trade organization is not a foreign-trade transaction, as *both* of the parties are of Soviet 'nationality'. Hence, the Soviet legal rules for foreign-trade transactions do not apply to such agreements. So far such agreements have not been practised, but it is conceivable that commissioning and purchase contracts might gain wide currency in these cases.

Internal Economic Turnover. The normative acts of 1987 treat JEs as fully-fledged parties in the economic turnover within the Soviet Union, guided by the premise that a JE enjoys the same legal status under civil law as other parties in economic relationships in the USSR. Special rules for JEs apply only in a few instances.

The most important sphere of the activity of a joint enterprise within the USSR is its daily contacts in the Soviet market, where it sells its products and purchases raw materials and other requirements. It functions within the USSR and, as necessary, enters into relationships with other enterprises and organizations operating in the domestic market. Decree 49 contains a fundamental provision laying the foundation for such contacts and concerning the realization of a joint enterprise's products in the Soviet market and deliveries to a joint enterprise from this market of equipment, raw materials, component manufactures, fuel, power and other products (para. 26).

Under Soviet legislation, upon agreement with other Soviet enterprises and organizations, a joint enterprise may determine the type of currency to be used for payment for sales and purchases of commodities, as well as the procedure for selling its products in the Soviet market and for deliveries from this market.

Material and technical supplies for joint enterprises (in particular raw materials, equipment and machine-building products) are effected on the basis of contracts signed with the respective Soviet foreign-trade organizations.

Decree 74 of the USSR State Committee for Supplies of 4 June 1987 approved the 'Procedure for providing material and technical supplies for joint enterprises established in the Soviet territory with the participation of other countries and foreign firms and marketing their products'.[2] This decree states that supplies for joint enterprises from the Soviet market of local materials and services are made in accordance with contracts with the territorial agencies of the USSR State Committee for Supplies and other local economic organizations. The content of such contracts is determined by a joint enterprise and a Soviet supplier, since there is no special proviso for another procedure. Such contracts are regulated by the general rules of Soviet civil law.

As a result material and technical supplies for joint enterprises and marketing of their products are effected through various channels: through Soviet foreign-trade organizations, through the wholesale trade system, through the supply system of the corresponding branches of the national economy, through retail trade and, finally, through direct contracts. The ensuing payments can be made not only in roubles but also in foreign currency.

Another sphere of major importance for the activities of a joint enterprise in the internal economic turnover is settlement of accounts. A JE's money resources in roubles are deposited in a rouble account in the USSR State Bank (Gosbank) and spent for the JE's purposes (para. 29, part 1). This means that a JE must be a party to an account agreement.

In this respect a joint enterprise is in the same position as any other

Soviet enterprise or organization. Gosbank is the national accounting centre which settles payments between all Soviet enterprises, organizations and agencies for commodities, services and the like. In accordance with the terms of an account agreement entered into with Gosbank an organization places money in an account with Gosbank and makes payments through Gosbank, while the latter is obligated to accrue to such account the amounts received from the account holder and other organizations, to hold such amounts and to execute the requests of the account holder. Money is debited from the account only with the consent of its holder, who makes payments for goods and services payable under various contracts. One of the principles for settling these accounts is clearing payments, that is the amounts transferred from the payer's account to the payee's account in a bank.

Of major importance for a joint enterprise is the problem of credits. Decree 49 is based on the premise that a joint enterprise may participate in this sphere of turnover. Like other participants in the economic turnover, it may obtain credits only from a bank. Unlike other Soviet participants in internal economic turnover, however, for a JE this includes not only Gosbank but also Vnesheconombank (para. 27 of Decree 49).

Regulation of a bank loan agreement involving a joint enterprise is based partly on general provisions, partly on special rules. In general a bank is entitled to control the use of credits. The same principle also applies to a joint enterprise. Decree 49 grants Gosbank and Vnesheconombank the right to effectuate control over the designated use, provision and timely repayment of credits issued to a joint enterprise (para. 28).

In contrast to the rules applicable to credits to other parties in the economic turnover, Decree 49 states that a joint enterprise 'may, when necessary, use credits obtained on commercial terms' (para. 27). On 22 September 1987 Gosbank and Vnesheconombank approved the 'Procedure for crediting and effecting settlements of joint enterprises, international amalgamations and organizations of the USSR and other CMEA countries, as well as joint enterprises with the participation of Soviet organizations and of firms from capitalist and developing countries'.[3]

Decree 49 recognizes a joint enterprise as a potential party to civil engineering projects. The decree states that the designing and capital construction of JEs' installations (including objects of social designation) are effected under contracts with their own funds or borrowed funds (para. 34). By virtue of this provision a JE may be a party to a turn-key contract. Such a contract could provide that the contractor (for example a special civil engineering organization) is obliged to build, by its own means and resources, a project conforming to approved design-and-estimate documentation and within a stipulated term, while the customer is obliged to provide a construction site, to transfer the approved design-and-estimate documentation, to secure the timely financing of the project, to accept commissioned projects and to pay for them. A turn-key contract under Soviet law is a *planned agreement*, a fact evidenced by the terms of Decree 49. The decree requires that a project's design be approved prior to the implementation of the project. The clearing procedure for the plans is established by the USSR State Committee for Construction (para. 34).

Decree 49 equates a joint enterprise with other Soviet parties in the economic turnover in matters pertaining to cargo transportation. The decree states that 'carriage of goods of joint enterprises shall be effectuated in the procedure established for Soviet organizations' (para. 35). Hence a joint enterprise may be a party to freight transport agreements on a par with other Soviet enterprises and organizations.

The comparative status of a joint enterprise in matters of insurance has also changed. According to Decree 49, 'the property of a joint enterprise shall be subject to compulsory insurance at insurance agencies of the USSR' (para. 14). Until recently compulsory insurance of property was binding only for a limited range of enterprises, namely those operating in agricultural production. This included state farms, other state agrarian enterprises and collective farms. At present compulsory insurance embraces the property of enterprises which have been transferred to new management methods.

In this regard JEs are in the same position as the overwhelming majority of other Soviet enterprises: JEs must conclude insurance contracts by force of law. Decree 49 stipulates that the risks of a JE are insured by agreement between the parties to the JE (para. 14).

NOTES

[1]   *Sobraniye postanovleniy SSSR*, Art. 35, No. 6, 1978.
[2]   *Foreign Trade*, No. 1, 1988, p. 45.
[3]   Ibid., pp. 45–6.

1992 SUPPLEMENTARY COMMENTARY

New Soviet legislation has completely decided the question of whether a joint enterprise is the owner of property formed out of the contributions of the participants.

The contribution of a foreign investor to the property of the JE during the JE's creation is regarded as a form of foreign investment. Foreign investments are not subject to nationalization, except in the case where such nationalization is effected in accordance with legislative acts of the USSR and the republics. In a case of nationalization, and in accordance with principles of international law which have now gained universal recognition, the foreign investor must receive *'prompt, adequate and effective'* compensation. The compensation must be paid without unsubstantiated delay, and it must correspond to the real value of the investment at the moment of adoption of the decision on nationalization. It is worth noting that the compensation must be paid in foreign currency and, at the wish of the investor, must be transferred abroad. Disputes concerning compensation are settled in USSR courts in accordance with legislative acts of the USSR and the republics. Where provided by international treaties (for example, as under the bilateral investment protection treaty between the USSR and Great Britain), or where otherwise agreed upon between the parties, such disputes may also be decided by international arbitration. In the case of arbitration the investor may refer the dispute to a standing artbitration body, such as the Arbitration Institute of the USSR Chamber of Commerce, or to an ad hoc arbitration panel, composed by special agreement of the parties or, for example, in accordance with the rules of UNCITRAL (United Nations Commission on International Trade Law). In other words the USSR has applied means of dispute resolution generally accepted in international practice to the system of investment disputes in the USSR.

The property of an enterprise with foreign investment may be used by it in order to secure any type of obligation, including the collateralization of loans. For this purpose the enterprise may use rights to buildings, structures and equipment, as well as other property rights, including possession and use of land.

In relation to economic activities in the USSR, joint enterprises have the right on a contract basis to establish the prices of their products (goods and services), to determine the manner of realization thereof on the domestic market and to select the suppliers of products (goods and services) from this market.

Careful attention should be paid to the changes effected in Soviet law on the issue of conflicts of laws. Most importantly the reader should note that in the Fundamental Principles of Civil Legislation of the USSR and Republics of 1991, a special rule has been included on the law governing agreements on the creation of joint enterprises. In accordance with paragraph 3 of Article 166, 'the law of the country where the joint enterprise has been founded shall apply to a contract concerning the creation of a joint enterprise with the participation of foreign juridical persons and citizens'. The rule is thus formulated that free choice of law by the parties to an agreement on the creation of a joint enterprise is not allowed.

Regarding relations between a JE and other natural and legal persons in connection with foreign economic transactions, the governing law may be chosen by the parties to such transactions. In the absence of such agreement the governing law is chosen for the parties by Article 166, depending on the type of contract in question.

III

Procedure for Establishing Joint Enterprises

Soviet legislation specifies the registration procedure for establishing joint enterprises in the USSR between Soviet organizations and firms from foreign countries. Paragraph 1 of Decree 49 of the USSR Council of Ministers of 13 January 1987 specifies that JEs may be established on the territory of the USSR solely on a licensing principle which shapes a definite system of preparing proposals on founding JEs and obtaining licenses. The Soviet partner (which can be any Soviet organization) interested in forming a JE negotiates directly with a foreign partner and prepares a feasibility report setting forth the economic reasons justifying establishment of a particular JE. At the initial stage of negotiations the parties may sign letters of intent (or 'protocols of intent') which recite their intention to found a JE.

During the following stages of negotiations, the parties draft foundation instruments. These will include a foundation agreement and a charter. The proposal on setting up the JE, together with the draft foundation instruments and the feasibility study, are submitted by the Soviet partner to the ministries and departments to which it belongs.

Originally Decree 49 required that the establishment of a JE be authorized by the USSR Council of Ministers. Subsequently, however, Decree 1074 of 17 September 1987 accorded the right to authorize JE establishment to the separate ministries and departments of the USSR and the Councils of Ministers of the Union republics.

As mentioned earlier in this book, the development of economic democracy in the USSR has considerably expanded the involvement of Soviet enterprises in external economic activity. It was specifically decreed that state enterprises, amalgamations and organizations may take decisions on establishing JEs jointly with foreign companies provided they have obtained the consent of their superior authority. It is obviously expedient first to obtain such consent and then to conclude an agreement. If the parties address such a body after concluding an agreement, it is advisable to allow for sufficient time for the superior authority to consider the agreement and give its reply according to Soviet legislation. While waiting for the reply (which may be negative) the parties should consider themselves free of any obligation to establish the JE.

Decree 49 itself does not contain any special provisions for the procedure of signing foundation agreements. Prevailing opinion considers that as a foundation agreement is a foreign-trade transaction, it must meet the requirement of two authorized signatures by the Soviet side (see above, Chapter II, section 2).

Decree 49 originally provided that the foundation agreement and charter should come into force after registration with the USSR Ministry of Finance. (*Editor's note*. The procedure for registration has changed considerably since the adoption of Decree 49 in 1987 and no longer takes place at the all-Union level; see, for example, Article 16 in Appendix 3.) From the moment of registration a JE acquires the rights of a juridical person. Registration of a JE is of major importance, for until then Soviet governmental, cooperative and economic organizations are forbidden to effect any transactions or sign any contracts with a JE. Soviet banks may open settlement and current accounts for JEs, extend credits and carry out credit-settlement clearing operations only after their registration.

To effect the JE's registration one of the partners (often the Soviet side) submits a written application, the aforementioned consent (or decision) of the superior authority and copies of the foundation instruments. Provided these meet established requirements the JE is recorded in a special register which sets forth the following information: the parties' foundation agreement, which body has approved the JE's establishment, the name of the Soviet partner and its higher authority, the name of the foreign partner and principle place of business, the objective of the JE's activity, the size of the JE's authorized capital and the shares of the partners.

A JE's liquidation is also subject to registration. According to Decree 49, 'a joint enterprise may be liquidated in instances and in the procedure stipulated by the foundation documents, and also by a decision of the USSR Council of Ministers if the activities thereof are not consistent with the objectives defined by these documents' (para. 51). We believe that the liquidation of a JE by decision of the USSR

Council of Ministers is an exceptional measure. (*Editor's note.* See Appendices 2 and 3.)

Agreements signed by the partners play a major part in solving essential problems related to the foundation of the JE and its operation. The first paragraph of Decree 49 stipulates that JEs are established '*on the basis of contracts concluded by participants of such enterprises*' (emphasis added).

The significance of the foundation instruments is manifest in the fact that in a number of its provisions Decree 49 specifies which matters pertaining to the foundation and operation of a JE shall be determined by these documents. These include: the definition of the object and purposes of the JE's activity (para. 7); its location (para. 7); the participants (para. 7); the size of the authorized capital (para. 7); the duration of its operation (para. 8); the composition and powers of its managerial bodies (para. 7); the procedure for decision-making by the management, primarily by its board (paras. 7 and 21); the procedure for transferring the rights to industrial property by the participants to the JE and vice versa (para. 17); legal protection of the rights to industrial property abroad (para. 17); the procedure for commercially exploiting the rights to industrial property (para. 17); the opening of branches and representations (para. 19); the procedure for defining the size of annual deductions from profits into the reserve fund (para. 30); the listing of the JE's assets, their formation and expenditure (para. 30); depreciation charges (para. 33); the furnishing of participants with data for exercising their controlling rights (para. 44); the content of collective contracts (para. 47); and the JE's liquidation procedure (paras. 7 and 51).

The above enumeration is not exhaustive. The agreement and the charter may, and indeed should, incorporate provisions on other matters related to the foundation and operation of the JE.

We may draw a conclusion that at the present initial stage of creating JEs in the USSR legislative regulation is limited to a narrow range of the most important and fundamental matters, so that a wider range of matters may be determined by the JE's participants. Contractual regulation therefore acquires a decisive significance.

However, the freedom of contractual discretion of the parties should not be understood in the way some analysts treat Soviet legislation in the West. Certain analysts, for example, believe that JE foundation instruments could include provisions incorporating a foreign state's legislation on joint stock and other companies. Thus, T. Schweisfurth of the Federal Republic of Germany assumes that this could be done if both sides were so willing.[1] Soviet legislation does not currently provide for such forms as a joint stock society or a society with limited responsibility. Therefore in our opinion an attempt to apply such forms within JE foundation instruments would be invalid. As for applicable law we can speak only about Soviet legislation, a question which we will consider further on. (*Editor's note.* Legislation on joint stock societies was adopted by the USSR and RSFSR subsequent to the above discussion.)

In practice, we distinguish between *preliminary agreements* and *foundation agreements* of a JE. The former imply 'protocols (or letters) of intent', which in general express the willingness of the parties to commence (or continue) negotiations on the establishment of a JE. Preliminary agreements merely declare the intention of the parties to set up a JE. Such agreements contain no property obligations of the parties. Often, however, they do oblige the parties to keep their negotiations confidential. Preliminary agreements also often stipulate the period during which the sides' intention to set up a joint enterprise will remain valid.

A foundation agreement is not necessarily preceded by a preliminary agreement. Moreover, a party may not demand the obligatory conclusion of a preliminary agreement.

Decree 49 does not specify which provisions must be included in the foundation agreement itself. However, it is logical for the parties to address in such agreements all the basic provisions which are vital for the JE's operation. First, such agreements define the parties, that is the partners in the prospective JE, designate the enterprise in Russian and a foreign language, its location and the object and purposes of its operation.

For example, the agreement could state that a JE is being founded to develop technologies and manufacture products on the basis of advances in science and technology, engineering know-how and production capacities of the partners. Reference may be made in this connection to the foundation documents (signed on 11 June 1987) of the first Soviet–Japanese Igirma–Tairiku enterprise in the Irkutsk region for the annual production of 90,000 cubic metres of lumber. The Soviet side undertook to provide the civil engineering work, raw materials, power resources, transportation of raw materials and finished products and utilities for contractual prices. The Japanese side undertook to supply the complete plant and machinery, equipment for the buildings, spare parts, tools and various materials for operational requirements; it was also to carry out contract supervision and adjustment and alignment work.[2]

The foundation agreement should also specify the life of the JE. Different options are possible in this regard. The parties might determine a definite period (often 20-30 years) and stipulate that that period may be prolonged. In the alternative they could state that the JE is established for an indefinite period of time.

A JE foundation agreement differs in its content from a JE charter. The latter specifies the object and purposes of the JE, its location, its partners, the size of the authorized fund, the size of the partners' shares, the order of making contributions to capital (including its foreign exchange part), the structure, composition and powers of its managerial bodies, the procedure for decision-making, the range of issues which can be settled by consensus and liquidation procedure. The charter may also incorporate other provisions. It is a supplement to the agreement. Together with other supplements it constitutes an indispensable part of the agreement. In case of discrepancies the provisions of the agreement rank higher than those of the charter. Some agreements specify this rule.

The basic provisions of the foundation agreement are usually repeated in the charter. The agreement reflects, however, the dynamics of a JE's establishment and development, while the charter is written in a static vein. This principle often determines which of the documents should include a certain provision.

The foundation agreement should pay greater attention to the rights and obligations of the parties arising from the foundation of the JE, while the charter should reflect its activities. The agreement may specify, for example, the Soviet participant's obligation to undertake all necessary registration formalities. The Soviet partner may also undertake in the agreement to secure the rights to use land, water and other natural resources and to lease equipment, premises, transport and communications. Conversely the foreign participant may be obligated to render assistance in training the Soviet personnel, in staffing the foreign personnel, in evaluating the world market, in exporting the JE's products and in performing similar functions.

As a rule all foundation agreements and charters specify that the JE is a juridical person, that it is established and operates in accordance with Soviet legislation, the agreement and the charter.

Agreements generally specify the manner of forming a JE's authorized capital and the parties' ensuing obligations. The parties' contributions to capital may also be listed in a special supplement to the agreement.

Agreements also briefly define the JE's managerial bodies, including its board, directorate (executive body) and audit commission. But these matters are often more detailed in a charter. The agreement determines, primarily, the composition of such bodies.

The charter usually specifies the exclusive powers of the board, which is entitled to make changes in the charter, to define the basic policies of the JE, to approve its plans, to increase or reduce its capital and the like. To be approved a decision on any of such matters requires unanimity. It will be noted that Decree 1405 adopted by the USSR Council of Ministers on 2 December 1988 states in plain words that the principal questions concerning a JE's activity are considered at the board's sessions on the basis of consensus. The charter defines the functions of the directorate, in particular of the director-general (chief executive officer), the audit commission, the JE's personnel, its official and working languages. As a rule the official languages are the languages of both parties, while the working language is usually Russian, although one JE set up in Estonia, for example, had three working languages – Russian, Finnish and Estonian. A provision stipulating the extent of liability of the parties for non-fulfilment of their obligations is also a normal feature of an agreement.

In the event of default or improper performance of a party's obligations that party is bound to compensate the losses sustained by the other party. Indirect losses and gains, in particular lost profit, are not liable to compensation.

It is expedient to specify such rules in a foundation agreement. It is also advisable to include provisions for *force majeure* in the agreement.

The procedure for settling disputes is another characteristic feature of such agreements. Under Soviet legislation disputes between the partners on a JE's operation are considered in Soviet courts of justice or, upon agreement between the parties, by a commercial arbitration tribunal (para. 20 of Decree 49).

From the above provision we may conclude that where parties fail to stipulate the manner of settling disputes, the latter are automatically considered in Soviet courts of justice. If the parties do stipulate the procedure for dispute settlement, they should specify which arbitration court will examine their disputes, rather than merely repeat the text of paragraph 20.

The above provision implies, first, that when signing an agreement the parties may specify that disputes, if any, shall not be taken to Soviet courts of justice, since the parties have agreed upon an arbitration procedure for settling disputes which excludes such courts' jurisdiction. Second, the parties may choose any arbitration procedure, which in our opinion might entail any number of procedures.

The parties may agree upon resolving their disputes in one of the standing arbitration tribunals or arbitration courts, for example, the Arbitration Court (formerly the Foreign Trade Arbitration Commission) attached to the USSR Chamber of Commerce and Industry. A number of foundation agreements already signed specify arbitration in this tribunal, while other agreements stipulate arbitration in a respondent's country.

May a dispute be submitted for consideration to any standing arbitration body in a third country? Of course, it is up to the parties to decide; there are no restrictions on the matter (as distinct from court proceedings). The USSR Chamber of Commerce and Industry has concluded agreements with the chambers of commerce of other states or arbitration associations which recommend that parties stipulate arbitration in a respondent's country. Such agreements were signed with India, Japan and several other countries. Similar specifications have been made in separate bilateral agreements on general commodity delivery terms (for example with Yugoslavia).

Nevertheless, it is our opinion that the most rational way to settle disputes between partners in a JE is by arbitration within the USSR. This judgement is based on the premise that a JE is a Soviet legal entity, and all the problems arising from its foundation and operation should come under Soviet law rather than that of any other country. The Soviet Union is the country where the JE is established and where it carries out its economic activity.

The procedure for dispute settlement is linked to applicable law. Soviet legislative acts on JEs themselves (for example Decree 49) contain no specific provisions on this issue. In our opinion a foundation agreement should specify the law applying to all matters involved in the establishment and operation of a JE in the USSR. The laws applied to the foundation agreement should be those applied to the JE itself, which is Soviet legislation. Some foundation agreements have already stipulated the applicable law. For example, a number of

Soviet JE foundation agreements have specified that questions arising in connection with the breach (or threatened breach) of such agreements, as well as questions with respect to such enterprises and their operations, shall be decided under Soviet legislation.

But the absence of such stipulation should not mean that another country's law should apply to the enterprise or to the relationships between the parties arising from the foundation agreement. In such relationships all rights and obligations of the JE partners arise from the establishment, operation or liquidation of a JE which, being located in the territory of the USSR, is a Soviet legal entity bound by Soviet laws. Therefore, if the parties have not expressly chosen which law shall apply, then in our opinion a court or arbitration should apply Soviet legislation to the relationships between the parties. Less appropriate would be reference to the rules governing the choice of laws contained in Article 126 of the 1961 Fundamentals of Civil Legislation, although the same result would probably be achieved. Article 126 provides that for a foreign trade transaction shall be governed by the law of the *place* of the transaction. In the case of the establishment of a JE in the USSR the transaction would be made in the USSR.

It would be even more inappropriate in our opinion to recommend that the contractual parties provide for the application of the law of any other third country, for example Swedish law. We think that neither Sweden nor any other country would have any essential link with the relations which arise from the creation and operation of a JE in the territory of the USSR. However, it is another matter to recommend application of another country's law in connection with transactions in goods or services for a JE from another country to the USSR or from the USSR to such country.

(*Editor's note*. The above discussion was written prior to the adoption in 1991 of new Fundamental Principles of Civil Legislation of the USSR and the Republics. The new Fundamental Principles explicitly provide that agreements on the foundation of joint enterprises with foreign participation are governed by the law of the country where such enterprises are founded.)

In view of the above conclusion on the importance of contractual regulation it is necessary to assess the correlation between Soviet legislative rules and provisions of the foundation instruments. May the provisions of agreements and charters *differ* from the rules of domestic Soviet legislation? Are these documents *lex specialis*, and do their provisions enjoy *priority* over those of general Soviet legislation on JEs?

This matter should be regarded from two viewpoints. First, may the foundation instruments incorporate provisions differing from the imperative norms of Soviet legislation? Second, do prospective changes in Soviet legislation bear upon the provisions of foundation instruments which treat some matters in a different way?

As regards the first question it would be advisable to analyze the general theory of Soviet law. The history of legal regulation in this field is of certain relevance, so it might be helpful to begin with a short historical outline.

The decree of the Council of People's Commissars (signed by V.I. Lenin on 23 November 1920) on the general economic and legal terms of concessions specified that 'the USSR government guarantees a concessionaire the inadmissibility of unilateral changes through any directives or decrees in the terms of concessionary contracts' (para. 6).[3]

The Main Concessionary Committee under the USSR Council of People's Commissars, founded in 1923, was empowered *inter alia*, to examine draft charters of joint stock societies based on concessionary contracts or exceptions from general laws, as well as draft charters of joint stock societies founded with the participation of foreign capital. All such drafts had to be submitted for approval by the USSR Council of People's Commissars, that is by the USSR government.[4]

In 1927 Regulations for Joint Stock Societies were adopted in the USSR. The decree of the Central Executive Committee and the Council of People's Commissars of 17 August 1927, which approved these regulations, specified that the provisions of charters of joint stock societies running contrary to the new Regulations for Joint Stock Societies (para. 6) were declared null and void, and the corresponding rules of the regulations should be applied instead. At the same time the decree stated specifically that 'in relation to joint stock societies whose charters have been approved in the concessionary manner and to other societies whose charters have been approved by the Council of People's Commissars or the Central Executive Committee of the USSR, the Regulations for Joint Stock Societies and the present decree are binding only in that part which does not contradict the charters of the said societies' (para. 11).[5]

Regarding the question at hand, of great interest is the fact that the regulations of 1927 confirmed the previously established procedure for approving the charters of joint stock societies with the participation of foreign firms by the USSR Council of People's Commissars. Article 12 specified that the Council of People's Commissars, on the report of the Main Concessionary Committee, approves the charters of societies in the following cases: (*a*) if the society is founded with the participation of foreign citizens or foreign juridical persons, or if the charter of a joint stock society provides for an opportunity for foreign citizens or foreign juridical persons to acquire its shares; (*b*) if the charter of a society, albeit founded without the participation of foreign capital, is of a concessionary character.[6]

After the enactment of the Fundamentals of Civil Legislation of 1961 and the Fundamentals of Civil Legal Proceedings in 1962, the Regulations for Joint Stock Societies of 1927, among other legislative acts, were abrogated. The charters of some organizations which were set up in the USSR in the form of joint stock societies (Foreign Trade Bank of the USSR)[7] were approved, after the abrogation of the general legislative act in each separate case by a decree of the USSR Council of Ministers. The participation of foreign capital in these joint stock societies was not permitted. Like the legal status of an earlier established joint stock society (Intourist), the legal status of such societies in the absence of a law on joint stock societies is determined by the general norms of civil legislation and the charters of the societies themselves.

As noted above, initially a JE's foundation instruments came into force after obtaining permission of an authorized governmental body. Such permissions usually took the form of an ordinance of a Union ministry or of the council of ministers of a Union republic. In our opinion such an ordinance can be considered an individual act of an administrative body. In principle though, such acts may incorporate provisions different from general acts only if they are approved by the same administrative body. But such provisions may be incorporated in the act itself of the administrative body rather than in the foundation instruments, since in contrast to the procedure existing in the 1920s the agreement itself and the charter are approved neither by the USSR government nor by any of its agencies. (Later, the system of obtaining a permission was replaced by a system of agreement.)

In approaching the above questions in terms of the content of foundation instruments we should underscore that all Soviet legislative regulations are divided into *imperative* and *supplementary*.[8] Imperative norms cannot be changed by parties to civil contracts. On the other hand, supplementary norms operate only inasmuch as the parties have not provided otherwise.

Decree 49 warrants that the charter of a JE may incorporate other provisions 'which are not contrary to Soviet legislation and which appertain to the peculiarities of the activities of the joint enterprise' (para. 7). Insomuch as substantively the nature of the terms of a foundation agreement and of the stipulations of a charter is identical, the above provision should be extended, in our opinion, to the foundation agreement.

Hence foundation instruments should never incorporate provisions contrary to the *imperative* norms of Soviet legislation. This conclusion can be corroborated by an additional argument concerning the correlation of JE foundation agreements with international agreements. Decree 49 specifies that a JE is guided in its activity by: (*a*) the Edict of 13 January 1987 of the Presidium, (*b*) Decree 49 itself and (*c*) 'other acts of legislation of the USSR and Union republics, with the exceptions established by inter-state and intergovernmental treaties of the USSR' (para. 1). This means that neither the charter nor the foundation agreement can incorporate provisions differing from the imperative norms. This is our answer to the first of the above questions.

The second question concerns the impact of prospective changes in Soviet legislation on JE foundation instruments. The Soviet state is interested in stable relationships between a JE's partners. With this in mind, we offer the following answer to the question: if new acts introduce changes bearing upon the status of a JE, the parties should have a reasonable opportunity to bring such changes into the terms of the agreement and adapt them to the changed circumstances. All the same the position of a foreign partner cannot be aggravated under any circumstances.

Previously, under Decree 49, the chairman and director-general of a JE's board were to be Soviet citizens. This provision was imperative for the partners to the agreement. Later, foreign citizens were also allowed to fill these positions (Decree 1405 of 2 December 1988). If a foreign participant now wishes that the board's chairman be a foreign citizen, then on agreement with the Soviet participant the parties should introduce appropriate changes in the foundation documents.

Soviet legislation provides definite guarantees for foreign investments in the USSR. Such guarantees may also be provided by international agreements – the Soviet Union is known for its positive attitude to such agreements. The practice of civil contracts should be consonant both with this premise of Soviet legislation and with the trend towards signing international investment protection agreements.

NOTES

[1] T. Schweisfurth, 'Die Rechtsgrundlagen für Gemein-schaftsunternehmen in der Sowjetunion', *Recht der internationalen Wirtschaft*, Issue 7, 1987, p. 491.

[2] *Ekonomicheskaya gazeta*, No. 26, 1987, p. 23.

[3] *Sobraniye uzakoneniy RSFSR*, Art. 181, No. 91, 1921.

[4] 'Decree on the foundation of the Main Concessionary Committee under the Council of People's Commissars of the Union of Soviet Socialist Republics of 21 August 1923', *Sobraniye uzakoneniy RSFSR*, Art. 952, No. 96, 1923.

[5] *Sobraniye zakonov SSSR*, Art. 499, No. 49, 1927.

[6] The functions of the Main Concessionary Committee as regards the preliminary examination of the drafts were provided for by the decree on concessions of 1931 (*Sobraniye zakonov SSSR*, Art. 27, No. 2, 1931).

[7] Decree of the USSR Council of Ministers of 7 June 1982 'On the approval of the statute of the Foreign Trade Bank of the USSR', *Sobraniye postanovleniy SSSR*, Art. 95, No. 18, 1982.

[8] *Theory of the State and Law* (Moscow, 1985), p. 324 (in Russian).

1991 SUPPLEMENTARY COMMENTARY

As noted above, since the adoption of Decree 49 in 1987 the procedure for creating joint enterprises in the USSR has not remained unchanged: it has undergone a process of both simplification and democratization. Legislation adopted in 1991 envisages that founders may independently decide to create a joint enterprise. In the case where the Soviet participant is a state enterprise the decision to create the JE is taken by its founders, with the consent of the owner of the state enterprise or its authorized organ. Moreover, Soviet citizens may also now act as participants in joint enterprises.

A vital change was effected to the procedure for registration. Beginning in 1991 JEs started being registered in accordance with procedures established by the individual republics. Thus, for example, in the RSFSR such enterprises are registered with the RSFSR Ministry of Finance or its authorized organs.

New legislation adopted in 1991 also resolved the question of guaranteeing foreign investors against future changes in legislation. In the event that future legislation of the USSR or its republics worsens the conditions of investing, then the legislation prevailing at the moment of investment will apply to it for ten years. However, this guarantee does not apply to changes affecting defence, national security, public order, taxation, credit and finance, environmental protection, the morality or health of the populace or anti-monopoly legislation.

IV

Joint Enterprise Foreign Economic Activities

1. Joint Enterprises in Production Cooperation

Economic cooperation in various forms has become a common phenomenon among enterprises from different countries. Such cooperation is especially significant for numerous countries in advancing their economies, not least because it serves them in attaining heightened levels of science, technology and production. Cooperation can also yield considerable material gains while saving time, since it helps to advance new branches in science and technology, boosting and modernizing production without any additional expenditure, on the basis of partners' achievements.

Cooperation is characterized by stable, and usually long-term, contacts between partners that can bring about even closer relationships and, in some instances, lead to joint enterprises, international amalgamations and organizations with different institutions, firms and management bodies from the participating countries. Such entities are often referred to in academic literature as 'joint economic organizations' (JEOs) and 'joint enterprises' (or JEs). (*Editor's note*. The JEO has been a form of economic cooperation among CMEA countries. The CMEA no longer exists as an inter-governmental organization, although economic relations among former CMEA countries continue, albeit at different levels.)

A shift from simple to more complex forms of cooperation is typical of economic integration. To cite but one example, we might consider the Soviet–Bulgarian research and production machine-tool amalgamation, Krasny Proletary–Beroe.

On 27 June 1985 the CMEA countries signed the General Agreement on cooperation in establishing joint specialized production of flexible machine-building systems and their extensive use in the national economies. In October that year the Soviet and Bulgarian governments signed an agreement on the foundation of Soviet–Bulgarian research and production amalgamations in machine-tool construction.

On the basis of those agreements an inter-departmental agreement was signed in Sofia in January 1986, with a view to setting up a Soviet–Bulgarian research and production amalgamation to manufacture digital control machine-tools, flexible production robots and manipulators. The Soviet party was represented by the Krasny Proletary production amalgamation, and the Bulgarian by the Beroe specialized plant and the computer-producing factory in Stara Zagora. By founding this particular JEO the USSR made a shift from cooperation on a contractual basis that did not entail new legal entities to a more complex form of international cooperation.

The Soviet–West German JE, Homatek, can serve as an example of how cooperation has resulted into closer links with companies from Western countries. It was founded in 1987 by the West German company Heinemann, which was engaged in the output of complex metal-working systems, flexible production modules and robotized complexes, and the Sergo Ordzhonikidze Machine-Tool Plant of Moscow. Previously the two parties had been cooperating on the basis of a mutual agreement on production and sales of goods, concluded in May 1986.[1]

Emerging as a result of longstanding cooperation, joint enterprises, international amalgamations and organizations can develop similar ties in science and technology, production, sales and technical services with other entities, including even the organizations responsible for founding the joint enterprise.

The main feature of a joint enterprise as a potential participant in international cooperation is that it has the status of a legal entity[2] and abides by the national law of the country in whose territory it is established (the 'host country'). The JE's legal status enables it to accomplish its task of organizing and carrying out economic activities in its respective field of operation over an extended period of time. Being a legal entity the JE is easily adaptable to the host country's economic and legal systems and becomes a part of its market structure.

Soviet institutions are becoming increasingly involved in a new type of cooperation. As an example, 1986 saw the Soviet and Bulgarian governments sign agreements on eight joint enterprises and 45 amalgamations and organizations. The same is typical of expanding economic cooperation between the Soviet Union and other of its traditional trading partners throughout Eastern and Central Europe.

Joint enterprises in various branches of these countries' economies will be essential for furthering international cooperation.

Joint enterprises are entitled to conclude agreements with both domestic and foreign entities. It stands to reason that any powers they possess, including the right to conclude agreements, are established by the national legislation of the host country, with exceptions ensuing from the nature of those enterprises, as well as by their own foundation instruments.

In this way joint enterprises can be regarded as a form of international cooperation in terms of joint production, which gives rise to a new legal entity engaged in the output of certain products. In its turn every legal entity has the necessary powers to enter into agreements with other legal entities of its level and, consequently, to act as a direct participant in relations based on cooperation.

Cooperation in general, and international cooperation in particular, is facilitated by establishing direct links between partners. As Soviet researcher Iu. Kormnov points out:

> International cooperation in the proper sense of the word demands wide-ranging exchanges in know-how and technology, joint efforts in science and technology, supplies of raw materials and stuffs and in coordinating the sales of products to the third countries. There is also the need for close connection between the prices of semi-finished products, units and spare parts and the final product. In this case, there is every reason to speak not only about interconnected production, but also about joint production, even if it is organized in different states and at factories belonging to different nations.[3]

According to Soviet legislation, Soviet institutions enjoy full powers in establishing direct links with foreign partners. Joint enterprises in the USSR are furnished with full powers to be used in establishing relations based on cooperation. For instance, under paragraph 6 of Decree 49 JEs may conclude agreements on their behalf, obtain property and personal non-property rights, meet their obligations and act as plaintiffs and defendants in courts of justice and arbitration.

Since cooperation is described as joint production, it is necessary to ensure an organized way of mutual deliveries of spare parts and units and finished products, as well as regular supplies of production with the necessary raw materials and stuffs, electricity and other components. Paragraph 26 of Decree 49 states as follows:

The procedure for the realization of products of a joint enterprise on the Soviet market and the delivery to the joint enterprise from this market of equipment, raw materials, materials, component manufactures, fuel, power and other products, as well as the type of currency connected with accounts for the realization of the product and goods purchased, shall be determined by the joint enterprise by agreement with the Soviet enterprises and organizations [as amended by Decree No. 352, 17 March 1988].

It was stated that a joint enterprise has the right to conduct independently export and import operations in line with its economic activities. These operations can also be carried out through Soviet foreign-trade organizations or the sales network of foreign participants on the basis of the relevant instruments.

Experience has shown, however, that this was an erroneous provision, especially in view of the joint enterprises' possible cooperation with Soviet organizations. To an extent it was corrected by Decree 1074 of the CPSU Central Committee and the USSR Council of Ministers, 'On additional measures to improve the country's external economic activity in the new conditions of economic management', adopted on 17 September 1987.

Previously, mutual supplies between joint enterprises and Soviet factories and organizations were to be paid for in roubles through relevant Soviet foreign-trade organizations, while, as Decree 1074 puts it, 'on agreement with Soviet factories and organizations, joint enterprises determine the type of currency in settling accounts for the sales and purchases, as well as the procedure of selling their products in the Soviet market and purchases from that market'.

This change may be regarded as a step forward in optimizing mutual contacts between joint enterprises and Soviet organizations, although it does not necessarily make the latter comply with the demands of the former and establish a different order in their cooperation, other than the one stated in Decree 49.

This conclusion is confirmed by the provision of Decree 1074 establishing the right of amalgamations, factories and organizations, ministries and departments of the USSR, as well as the councils of ministers of the Union republics to purchase products with payments from the available currency funds without any coordination with Soviet foreign-trade firms and offices. Such purchases are given priority and taken into account in fulfilling the plans of foreign-trade organizations.

In other words the decree means that all the sales and purchases made by Soviet factories and organizations using their currency funds (also from joint enterprises, since there is no reservation that the above provision does not apply to them) have to be coordinated with the relevant foreign-trade firms and amalgamations. This provision is essential in establishing the order of maintaining contacts between joint enterprises and their Soviet partners.

As a whole, new acts designed to regulate the activities of USSR-based joint enterprises provide greater opportunity (which has been used insufficiently so far) for such ventures to become part and parcel of both external and internal economic ties in the Soviet Union, including those based on cooperation.

Such economic ties which result in international division of labour may be beneficial to the Soviet economy, provided certain legal, financial and production adjustments are made with respect to the activity of joint enterprises as new legal entities in Soviet law.

2. *Foreign-Trade Activities of Joint Enterprises Set Up in the Soviet Union*

Foreign trade has been a traditional form of international economic relations and is constantly expanding. Even today it acts as an intermediary in maintaining production links between enterprises in different states exchanging their products on the basis of production cooperation.

Joint enterprises are a new form of economic cooperation, although they are closely linked to the traditional form, namely foreign trade. On the one hand joint enterprises are designed to extend the country's export potential and to boost the share of machinery and equipment in its export pattern. On the other hand they will also affect the import pattern – cutting down irrational imports of goods that can be produced on a domestic basis and yield profit is of no less importance than advancing exports. In this way, while serving to develop new forms of economic cooperation, foreign trade hinges upon the results of that cooperation.

Joint enterprises are generally designed, as their foundation instruments envisage, to develop joint production rather than engage in foreign-trade activities. Furthermore, some of the foundation agreements of these JEs contain a production programme as part of the agreement and take it as their goal to develop, manufacture and distribute competitive products. Foreign-trade operations are regarded as *ancillary* aspects meant to facilitate the normal functioning of production.

A joint enterprise is not included in the system of material and technical supplies of Soviet state enterprises; therefore, such JEs must conclude contracts for the supplies of raw materials, equipment and the like with either Soviet or foreign firms and factories. It should be borne in mind that the prices of Soviet goods for a JE of this kind will be fixed with regard to the world prices. Despite the well-founded concern over material and technical supplies expressed by foreign partners, JEs are successfully coping with this problem.

At the initial stages JEs must market their product with the help of foreign-trade amalgamations or through the marketing channels of their foreign partners upon concluding contracts, as Decree 49 envisages. At the later stages, when production organization is completed, JEs may consider the need for independent activity in the external market and set up the necessary branches and firms in the Soviet Union and agencies abroad. Regarding their imports they evidently may rely more on foreign participants (who may only gain from their financial successes).

Thus a number of these JEs count on receiving profits in hard currency through direct sales to their foreign participants. Such sales, which have to ensure the joint enterprises' self-sufficiency in currency, help alleviate currency problems they may face. At the same time these JEs also have the right to export their products to foreign markets independently or through foreign economic bodies.

It is noteworthy that, according to paragraph 31 of Decree 1405 of the USSR Council of Ministers of 2 December 1988, 'the goods imported to the Soviet Union by joint enterprises for the needs of their production are liable to minimal duties or can be exempt from duty'.

It is also noteworthy that some JE foundation instruments establish a division of markets. For instance, they have the right to sell their products in the internal market, while foreign participants have the right to distribute such products on the world market. The decree of 17 September 1987, adopted by the CPSU Central Committee and the USSR Council of Ministers, provides that JEs may agree with Soviet factories and organizations on the type of currency in accounts for their sales and purchases, as well as the rules of selling their products in the Soviet market and getting supplies from that market.

From this the conclusion may be made that JEs are entitled to market their products within the Soviet Union not only for roubles but also for hard currency. This provides yet another guarantee of availability of hard currency for distribution of profits to foreign participants and payment of other hard currency expenses, for example for purchases of foreign equipment. (*Editor's note.* Currency laws and regulations adopted in 1991 now regulate the instances in which hard currency may be used as a form of payment on the territory of the USSR.)

In our view the right to determine the currency for settlements meets the interest of both parties and, when necessary, allows sales of a substantial portion of a JE's products in the internal market without any detriment to the JE's currency plans.

JEs are independent of any quotas established for Soviet economic bodies. Since JEs are free to establish their own programmes of economic activity, they also have independent programmes of export and import. The size of exports and imports is determined by JEs depending on their opportunities and requirements, without mandates from state bodies.

In line with the 2 December 1988 Decree of the USSR Council of Ministers, all JEs founded in the USSR resolve key issues of their activities unanimously by the members of their respective boards. This serves as a guarantee for all participants in these JEs (para. 31).

Export and import licenses are essential for JEs in foreign-trade activities. Such permits are granted to them in accordance with the rules established in the Soviet legislation, in particular by Decree 1513 of the USSR Council of Ministers adopted on 22 December 1986. More specific details are contained in the inter-departmental instruction, 'On granting export and import licenses to and from the USSR of goods and other kinds of property and re-exports of goods', adopted on 27 March 1987. According to paragraph 24 of the instruction, JEs are granted annual general export and import licenses for goods needed in their activity.

In retrospect, some aspects of joint enterprises' foreign-trade activities should be identified:

1. Unlike other Soviet organizations, JEs set up in the USSR have a much wider scope of material responsibility. Thus in case of recovery on obligations, penalty is imposed on socialist organizations' financial

resources that are kept in banks (Art. 40 of the RSFSR Code of Civil Procedure). In case the money available is insufficient for the payment of debts the penalty may be imposed on the fixed assets of those organizations (for the state cost-accounting organizations, or property for public cooperatives), except for the assets or property exempt from penalty on the basis of Articles 98, 101 and 104 of the RSFSR Civil Code (Arts. 411–13 of the Code of Civil Procedure). Recovery is not allowed in respect to institutions, factories and organizations budgeted by the state (Art. 411, part 2 of the Civil Code).[6] On the contrary, 'a joint enterprise shall be liable for it obligations in all of its property' (para. 18, Decree 49). (*Editor's note.* The distinctions between Soviet state enterprises and JEs with foreign participation have been abolished.)

2. All JEs have the right to conduct operations in foreign markets both independently and with the help of foreign economic organizations.

3. As a juridical person a JE must abide by the USSR general and specific legislation of foreign trade in its foreign-trade activities. Primarily this concerns the signing of a transaction, contract liabilities and the like.

4. Joint enterprises may participate in foreign trade independently or through Soviet foreign-trade firms. Joint enterprises are reserved the right to sell their products through the foreign partners.

In this manner JEs have every possibility to make their products more competitive within accelerated periods of time, since they possess all the rights to participate in foreign trade, have advanced technology at their disposal and immediately use changes in internal and external market conditions to their advantage.

NOTES

[1] *Pravda*, 7 September 1987.
[2] Except for JEOs of the partnership type that do not have such status, for this type of JEO does not entail a new independent legal entity.
[3] *Legal Forms of Organizing Joint Enterprises by CMEA Countries*, (Moscow, 1985), p. 69 (in Russian).
[4] Iu. Kormnov, *Production Specialization and Cooperation in CMEA Countries* (Moscow, 1972), p. 92 (in Russian).
[5] Similar provisions are to be found in Decree 74 of 4 June 1987, adopted by the USSR State Committee for Supplies 'Procedure for providing material and technical

supplies for joint enterprises set up in the Soviet territory with the participation of other countries and foreign firms and marketing their products'.
6 *Commentaries to the RSFSR Civil Code* (Moscow, 1982), p. 61 (in Russian).

1991 SUPPLEMENTARY COMMENTARY

Since the adoption of the first normative acts concerning the creation of joint enterprises in the USSR, profound changes have occurred in Soviet regulation of foreign economic activities. The essence of these changes consisted of the following:
– all Soviet enterprises received the right to enter the foreign market;
– a system of qualification and licensing for all principle categories of goods and services was introduced; and
– a distribution of competence in the sphere of foreign economic activities was accomplished.

The Fundamental Principles of Legislation on Foreign Investments of 1991 established that JEs with foreign investment of 15 per cent or more have the right to export their own products (goods and services) without having to obtain a licence. (Legislation of the RSFSR on foreign investment gives such a right to enterprises with more than 30 per cent foreign investment.) Moreover, *all* enterprises with foreign investments have the right to import products (goods and services) for their own economic activities without having to obtain a licence.

Joint enterprises' receipts in foreign currency remain at their disposition.

Regarding assessment of customs duties, the exemption was preserved for all JEs from payment of customs duties on property imported into the USSR as part of a foreign investor's capital contribution to a JE charter fund. Additionally property imported into the USSR by foreign employees of a JE for their own personal needs is also exempt from customs duty.

V

Currency and Other Financial Issues in Connection with Joint Enterprise Operations

1. Currency and Other Financial Legislation of the USSR and Joint Enterprises

Joint enterprises with the participation of firms from foreign countries are a new phenomenon for the Soviet Union. Adaptation of this form of activity to Soviet national economic conditions raises the problem of establishing an adequate legal mechanism for regulating all aspects of relationships arising out of the activities of such enterprises. This raises the following questions: to what extent is current Soviet legislation ready for the emergence of a new economic subject – the JE; and what new legal instruments should be elaborated to regulate the activities of the JE?

It should be observed that Decree 49 and Decree 1074 (Decree 1405) provide for the most general approaches to regulating the above relationships. Their provisions, with a few exceptions, require additional clarification regarding their references to either Soviet national legislation or to corresponding international agreements.

Currency and other related financial problems arising out of joint enterprises' operations are among the most complicated issues, for on the one hand they touch upon the sphere of the currency monopoly of the Soviet state, and on the other they are directly linked with setting up such economic conditions which would benefit both the Soviet Union and partners from foreign countries.

The principal organizational activity aimed at securing the currency monopoly is exercised by Soviet banks, namely by the USSR State Bank (Gosbank) and the USSR Bank for Foreign Economic Affairs (Vnesheconombank). According to its statute, Gosbank engages in banking operations linked with the foreign trade of the Soviet Union, as well as in other transactions with currency valuables.[1] Its statute states that transactions in sales and purchases of currency valuables in the territory of the USSR are made exclusively by Gosbank. Other organizations enter into similar operations under the guarantee of Gosbank.

Gosbank's statute makes an exception for foreign trade which calls for a banking agency capable of independent regulation of relationships arising from the use of foreign currency. Vnesheconombank meets these requirements – it constitutes a centralized system undertaking all the key operations in the import, export, transfer and other uses of currency valuables in the Soviet Union. Vnesheconombank is founded in the form of a joint stock society, with Soviet organizations as its shareholders. Its operations are grounded either on mandates given by Gosbank or on terms of international treaties of the USSR with other states which direct Vnesheconombank to ensure cooperation thereunder.[2]

Apart from the above, the responsibility of Vnesheconombank for operations in a definite sphere of foreign economic contacts may also be specified in a legislative act (cf. para. 27, Decree 49). The role of Vnesheconombank under new conditions of economic management is considerably expanding in view of a noticeable increase in the scale of operations in export–import and non-commercial transactions and a wider scope of the Bank's activity in world currency and credit markets.[3]

Gosbank and Vnesheconombank will continue to settle accounts in foreign currency in the foreseeable future, but the state of affairs in the given sphere is expected to change somewhat in view of measures taken to streamline the external economic activity of the USSR. First of all, the establishment of joint enterprises, expansion of self-sustained state enterprises and establishment of foreign-trade associations at the industrial ministries give rise to new links in currency relationships, which enjoy considerable independence.[4]

The process is likely not only to extend the volume of currency operations but also to intensify the cooperation of Soviet banks with their foreign counterparts. The normative bases for such cooperation are found in various USSR legislative acts, which provide an opportunity for Soviet banks to sign agreements with foreign banks with a view to obtaining and granting services in currency transfers, obtaining credits and carrying out other banking operations.[5]

But now, besides banks, agreements with foreign banks can be concluded by JEs – with the consent of Vnesheconombank (para. 27, Decree 49). Thus a JE becomes one more organization possessing major reserves of foreign currency. Such foreign currency may make up a part of a JE's authorized capital (para. 11, Decree 49). It should be noted that demands of a JE in foreign currency must, as a rule, be satisfied by the earnings from sales of its products in the external market, though a JE could choose, upon agreement of Soviet enterprises and organizations, the type of currency to settle payments for products and commodities sold or purchased in the domestic Soviet market. (*Editor's note.* This rule has subsequently changed, and a JE's use of foreign currency is subject to new currency rules.)

The granting to a JE of the independent right to export and import as needed, along with the principle of currency self-support and the possibility of direct participation in international financial relationships, make for an extensive circulation of foreign currency through financial channels within the Soviet economy.

This trend presents two demands on legislators. First, legislators must revise and supplement the existing normative acts in view of the transformed mechanism of external economic activity of the Soviet state, primarily, such general acts as the Edict of the Presidium of the USSR Supreme Soviet, 'On transactions in currency valuables in the territory of the USSR'[6] and the Regulations for Import, Export, Transfer and Overseas Remittances of Soviet and Foreign Currency and Other Currency Valuables. We would remind readers that the edict on transactions in currency valuables defines the term 'currency valuables' as foreign currency, payment documents and securities in foreign currency, as well as banking payment documents in roubles acquired for foreign convertible currency and which can be converted into hard currency. All of these items are included in the property which may comprise a JE's authorized capital (para. 11, Decree 49). It is natural that the treatment of this property and the procedure for transactions with it will considerably differ from similar matters pertaining to other types of currency valuables in the Soviet territory. This differentiation should be reflected in normative acts.

The corresponding implementing regulations should be introduced through special acts (instructions, regulations of the USSR Ministry of Finance and the like). Separate issues arising from foreign currency circulation in the USSR are likely to be specified in normative acts regulating particular spheres of economic activity. Take, for example, paragraph 13 of Decree 49, which provides for customs duty exemptions for the property imported by a foreign partner for founding the authorized capital stock of a joint enterprise, and paragraph 34 of the decree of 2 December 1988, which provides benefits in taxation of goods imported for a JE's production development or compensation of employees.

The second demand on legislators arising out of more extensive circulation of foreign currency is to elaborate appropriate legal mechanisms to guarantee the Soviet economy against negative implications of utilizing convertible currency for national economic undertakings. Such utilization will inevitably provoke a certain impact of the cyclic performance of the world financial market on those branches of the Soviet economy dealing with the currency markets of capitalist countries. Soviet currency, the rouble, has been a domestic currency in the same measure as the currencies of the majority of socialist countries. Settlements among socialist countries have been effected by way of a common-payment unit, the foreign exchange rouble. The use of convertible currency in foreign trade practically has no effect on the Soviet domestic economy, as convertible currency permanently circulates in foreign trade (although the 2 December 1988 decree does provide for the introduction of currency settlements between socialist enterprises and charts measures on making the ruble convertible).

In the case of JEs we now encounter a scheme of interaction of national and foreign currencies, something fundamentally new for the Soviet economy. *Both* currencies may comprise an integral part of the authorized capital of a JE, and *both* may be used in its relationships with its partners, crediting agencies and other third parties. Such interaction of national and convertible currencies, as the experience of socialist countries testifies, raises a great number of problems. Such matters as, for example, the valuation of a foreign partner's contribution to the authorized capital may present difficulties, the solution to which offered by paragraph 12 of Decree 49 (the valuation of a foreign partner's contribution in Soviet roubles at the official Gosbank exchange rate prevailing on the day of execution of the agreement or such other date agreed upon by its parties) cannot be considered universal.

The problem of legal security of interacting national and freely convertible currencies within the framework of the property of JEs has yet not been resolved, not only in Soviet legislation undertaking the first steps in this respect but also in the laws of those other socialist countries which have had some experience in it.

A JE becomes a party to economic (including financial) relationships after its registration with the USSR Ministry of Finance, which then notifies the respective financial organ controlling the settlement of accounts between JEs and the state budget. Subsequently the JE's bank opens current and settlement accounts for the JE, makes funds available and carries out payment–credit operations with it. The extension of credits to JEs is made on commercial terms following the procedure specified by the corresponding legislative acts.[8]

Notably, paragraph 28 of Decree 49 specifically entitles Gosbank and Vnesheconombank 'to effectuate control over the designated use, provision and timely repayment of credits issued to the joint enterprise'. Thus such organs may control not only such credits as are obtained *within* the USSR (irrespective of the currency – in roubles or in foreign currency) but also the JE's financial activity in *external* markets.

A credit agreement between a JE and a bank should provide security for credits by submitting to the bank collateral on commodity–material and other valuables. If necessary a bank may demand mortgages on buildings, structures and other equipment.

For their currency deposits in Soviet banks JEs receive interest paid in foreign currency at rates prevailing from time to time on the world money market. Exchange rate differences with respect to the currency accounts of a JE and its operations in foreign currency are relegated to their profits and losses (para. 29, Decree 49). The currency received by a JE from foreign financial organs must be remitted to the Soviet Union in conformity with the Regulations for Import, Export, Transfer and Overseas Remittances of Soviet and Foreign Currency and Other Currency Valuables, which regulate such matters as transferring abroad sums in foreign currency, credit payments of JEs to foreign banks, currency exchange and the like.

In particular, the regulations stipulate the right of Gosbank and Vnesheconombank to transfer Soviet currency to the banks of those foreign countries which are a party to currency exchange agreements, as well as the right to make bank transfers overseas of foreign currency to the financial agencies of the states which are a party to the Agreement on Non-Commercial Payments (see Chapters IV and VII). We are of the opinon that, in view of the growing scope of currency operations arising from the activity of JEs, the grounds for remittance of foreign currency by Soviet banks will be broadly extended.

Payments of JEs to suppliers and customers in the USSR are made through foreign trade organizations, as a general rule, at world market prices. Nonetheless, in cases when the supplies and purchases are effected at current Soviet prices, the usual procedure applies, namely that provided for internal domestic payments. (*Editor's note*. Joint enterprises may now directly effectuate payments to suppliers and customers.)

It is noteworthy that in their dealings in foreign markets JEs carry out all export–import transactions in full conformity with the terms of their contracts and international banking practices. This includes payment of the commissions charged by overseas banks (in conformity with pre-established rules) for the services they render to JEs.

Under paragraph 6 of Decree 49, a JE is a legal entity according to Soviet legislation. This does not mean that the legal financial status of a JE lacks its own specific features. On the contrary, it is obvious that these enterprises act as new parties to financial legal relationships alongside state enterprises and associations, collective farms, cooperatives and public organizations. Their status is regulated by special provisions of legislative acts (for example the Edict of the Presidium of the USSR Supreme Soviet of 13 January 1987), while the non-specific questions of their financial status come under the jurisdiction of general legal acts regulating the financial legal relationships between Soviet economic organizations.

Paragraph 30 of Decree 49 provides for the establishment of a reserve and such other funds as are necessary for a JE's activity. The reserve fund is a new phenomenon in Soviet economy, although hereafter such funds are to be set up as state socialist enterprises also.[9] It was the legislators' belief that establishing a reserve fund in the amount of 25 per cent of authorized capital would protect the JE's normal functioning from fluctuations of economic conjunctures. The procedure for making deposits to the reserve fund (as well as any other funds) is established by JEs' constitutive instruments.

Paragraph 33 of Decree 49 stipulates the obligation of a JE to make amortization deductions in the manner established for Soviet state organizations, unless otherwise provided in the JE's constitutive instruments. The depreciation fund is used for overhaul and modernization of production, as well as for complete replacement of fixed assets. Between 10 and 50 per cent of the depreciation fund is allotted, under established standards, to the fund for the expansion of production, while the rest is spent for technical equipment and reconstruction. The money resources planned for overhaul are directed toward specific purposes and must be used for such purposes. The manner and terms of depreciation are determined by Soviet legislation with due account for the specific circumstances of a given enterprise. Similar terms for depreciation are established for JEs, although with respect to JEs these terms should be obviously somewhat adjusted, taking into account the specific features of their operations.

Budgetary payments of JEs only partially coincide with the obligations borne by Soviet enterprises under the state budget. In some respects provisions for taxation of JEs are similar to those established by law for collective farms, cooperatives and public organizations which pay taxes on actual target profit and excess profits taxes, that is taxes on sums accumulated as a result of income exceeding monetary expenditures.[10]

(*Editor's note.* Since the original adoption of Decree 49, the Soviet tax system has undergone considerable change, and JEs are no longer taxed under Decree 49 but under other applicable tax laws. Similarly the system of individual income tax, as well as that of social insurance and pensions, has also changed substantially. The following discussion on these issues has been retained for its historic significance.)

Several types of budgetary payments are established for state enterprises and amalgamations: standard turnover taxes, payments for the basic production assets, rental payments and payments of profit balance. The turnover tax paid by all state enterprises, cooperatives and public enterprises is levied on receipts out of sales of industrial products, by trading organizations, etc. Various methods of estimating the turnover tax exist, and rates depend on specific economic conditions in separate branches and enterprises.

In line with paragraph 36 of Decree 49, JEs pay an income tax in the amount of 30 per cent of the portion of the profits remaining after their distribution for the inner needs of the enterprise. The taxable income of a JE is determined as the difference between the balance profits and deductions into all the funds formed by the enterprise. It should be observed that the income tax levied on JEs is paid in roubles (paras. 6 and 10, Instruction 124 of the USSR Ministry of Finance 'On the taxation of joint enterprises' of 4 May 1987). Joint enterprises make no rental payments or payments for the fixed assets, and the balance of profits gained after the payment of income tax is distributed among the partners of a JE in proportion to their shares in the authorized capital. Paragraph 31 of the 2 December 1988 decree states that it is expedient to free JEs in the Far Eastern Economic Region from tax on profits during the first three years starting from the date the profits will be declared. Furthermore, the rate of income tax in the Far Eastern Economic Region is abated to 10 per cent, and the general rules of taxation may be adjusted to comply with the rules of other countries.

An extra 20 per cent tax is levied on part of the profits transferred abroad by a foreign partner (para. 3, Edict of 13 January 1987; para. 41, Decree 49; and para. 12, Instruction 124 'On the taxation of joint enterprises'). The JE does this by submitting an application to Vnesheconombank for transferring the profits abroad and simultaneously a money order for transferring to the state budget a tax in the currency of the transfer.

Taxation of the profits transferred abroad is one of the measures for stimulating reinvestments, which is justified in economic terms. The USSR Ministry of Finance is entitled to reduce the size of the income tax, the tax on profits transferred abroad, or exempt from taxes some payers. The Ministry of Finance should apply this rule mostly to JEs which manufacture consumer goods, medical technology and drugs as well as science-intensive products which are of primary importance for the national economy.[11] In such case, a JE should submit to the financial organ at the place of its location a well-grounded application for tax exemptions. Furthermore, the taxation of a JE may be changed by a treaty between the USSR and the corresponding country. On the whole, international treaties in the taxation sphere are likely to play a major role. Primarily such treaties will include agreements on general economic matters but may also include special documents regulating the taxation. To date the Soviet Union has cooperation agreements on taxation with a number of Western countries.

The most acute problem arising in this field is the elimination of double taxation levied on the incomes of partners in a JE. To avoid double taxation the appropriate conventions as a rule provide for single-state taxation for the following categories of profits: (*a*) payment, royalty or other remunerations for the use or the right to use inventions, production prototypes, technologies or formulas, software, trade marks, service marks and other similar property, or the payment for the use of production, trade, research equipment or know-how; (*b*) profits gained from the sales or exchange of such rights or property; (*c*) profits gained from sales or other disposals of inherited property; (*d*) profits yielded from granting engineering, architectural, design and other technical services under contract with a contract supervisor permanently residing in a given state at one project during a definite period of time; (*e*) profits from commodity sales or provision of services through a broker, commission agent or other independent agent if such activity is not contrary to such agent's functions; (*f*) bonuses for surplus insurance operations; (*g*) interest on credits for the trade operations between the USSR and its partners, except for the interest received by a person residing in another state on routine banking operations in that state.[12]

Besides, single-state taxes are levied on profits gained from international air and sea transportation and also on dividends and interest, with several exceptions stipulated by international conventions. The latter provision may apply to JEs in the form of 'joint stock societies', in the event that this becomes an allowable form of organization in the Soviet Union in the future.

Moreover, the texts of some conventions include articles stipulating that all types of income not incorporated in the listing provided by a given convention are subject to taxation only in the country of a legal entity's permanent residence. This important provision might be applied to taxation of JEs until these matters become specially regulated.[13] The relevant conventions also specify the procedure under which states should provide for double taxation exemptions in conformity with national legislation in cases when the income of a legal entity is formally subject to taxation in both countries.[14]

With respect to a JE's tax payments, international agreements may provide for exemptions regarding both the income tax of a JE itself and tax obligations of its separate employees. These exemptions are specified either in international agreements or in special legislation regulating the activity of JEs. As for the income tax of JEs, paragraph 36 of Decree 49 specifies that JEs are exempt from taxes on their profits during the two initial years of their operations, with exceptions stipulated in relevant laws (for example para. 31, Decree of 2 December 1988). The two-year period is calculated from the moment the JE receives the profits declared.[15]

The conventions provide for special tax exemptions for persons engaged in some definite types of activity. These include income gained by government officials from their official duties at places of permanent residence during their stay in another state; lecturers' wages, students' and apprentices' scholarships; and fees received by persons engaged in inter-governmental cooperation projects. Whether such categories would in fact be applicable to the foreign personnel of a JE would, of course, depend upon the circumstances in a given instance.

The wages of foreign citizens employed by a JE, as specified in paragraph 50 of Decree 49, are taxed in the manner stipulated in the Edict of the Presidium of the USSR Supreme Soviet of 12 May 1978, 'On the income tax levied on foreign legal and natural persons'. This edict states that all the incomes of foreign natural persons gained from their activity in the USSR are taxed in the manner and measure established by Soviet legislation for Soviet citizens. Consequently a progressive income tax is levied on wages and other sums stipulated in paragraph 11 of the Decree of 12 May 1978 and received by personnel of a JE.[16]

Decree 49 and the Instruction 'On the taxation of joint enterprises' specify the cases of a JE's liability for arrears of tax payments. A JE pays a pecuniary fine in the amount of 0.05 per cent for each delayed day (para. 39, Decree 49, and para. 11, Instruction 'On the taxation of joint enterprises'). The collection of delayed tax payments is carried out in the manner established for foreign legal entities by the Regulations for Collecting Delayed Taxes.[17] These regulations specify that collection of arrears from foreign legal entities may be executed only by a court's judgement (para. 12).

A rule is also provided according to which in separate cases an outstanding debtor could be granted a delay in tax payments, with a pecuniary fine or without it, depending on the judgement of a collector. The surplus in tax payments could be returned to a tax payer or reckoned towards future tax payments in case less than six months have expired since the court's judgement on the tax collection.

In addition to the above deductions JEs make payments to the USSR national budget for the social insurance of Soviet and foreign personnel and for old-age security of Soviet employees at rates established by Soviet legislation for Soviet state enterprises (para. 49, Decree 49).

Normative acts specify the procedure for social insurance dues to be paid by the tariffs established by the USSR Council of Ministers for the various categories of manual and office workers. These dues are charged from the gross wages (including additional payments, bonuses, premiums and other remunerations provided for by the wages system) of manual and office workers, and other categories of employees who are entitled to social insurance. Specific types of payments in social insurance are determined by the All-Union Central Council of Trade Unions upon coordination with the USSR State Committee of Labour and Social Affairs and the USSR Ministry of

Finance.[18] Payments for retirement security of the foreign personnel, as specified in paragraph 49 of Decree 49, are made to the corresponding funds of countries of their permanent residence, in the respective currency.

The above rule is the last one in the range of matters pertaining to the financial status of a JE in the USSR. On the whole, we should note that the norms regulating the currency and financial issues arising from JEs' operations are further specified in special legislative acts. Furthermore, we should also stress once more that in the regulation of currency and financial aspects of JEs' performance an exceptional role is attached to the constitutive instruments, primarily the agreement on the foundation of a JE.

2. *Forms of Controlling the Activity of Joint Enterprises*

The establishment and operation of JEs raise a number of problems, one of the most serious of which is the control over their activity in the territory of the USSR.

A separate examination of this problem is explained primarily by the apprehension of foreign partners, especially those from capitalist countries, of active interference and control on the part of the state over the activity of joint enterprises. Such suspicions are evident with respect to other socialist countries also, when considering whether or not to found a joint enterprise in their territory.

Therefore, a clear-cut formulation of normative provisions regulating the rights and obligations of partners in a JE and the rights of Soviet governmental bodies to control JEs' activity should help overcome the existing fears of foreign partners.

The forms of controlling the activities of JEs, and the procedure, manner and methods of exercising such control, are outlined in the decrees of the Soviet government only in general terms, which naturally requires additional concrete expression. First, partners in a JE themselves are charged with the prime supervisory functions. Thus paragraph 41 of Decree 49 specifies that partners in a JE, to exercise their rights to supervision, are furnished, in the manner stipulated in its constitutive instruments, with the data on its current operations, its property, profits and losses, audits being carried out as agreed upon (para. 33, USSR Council of Ministers Decree 1405 of 2 December 1988).

Joint enterprises may establish an audit commission in the manner specified in their constitutive instruments. For example, the statute of a JE may stipulate that an audit commission will be appointed by its board to check its financial, economic and commercial activities. The board would then examine and approve the reports and conclusions such commission would draw from periodic audits.

It should be noted that there are no such commissions in Soviet state enterprises. Audit commissions are, however, established in cooperatives, public organizations and in collective farms. As a rule, audit commissions are established with a view to controlling the economic and financial activity, maintenance of the property, and supervision of the observance of contractual terms and economic operations and the like.

The main purpose of an audit commission formed in a JE is to monitor for violations of economic and financial discipline and to remove the cause thereof.

The verification of the financial–economic and commercial activity of JEs could be effectuated by a Soviet auditing organization. In September 1987 the joint stock society Inaudit was established in Moscow with a view to according auditing and consultation services to JEs operating in the USSR and abroad with the participation of Soviet organizations, as well as to organizations and agencies dealing with foreign currency in the USSR and overseas.

Inaudit has its own statute, being a juridical person acting on the principles of cost-accounting. It checks the commercial and economic–financial operations of JEs, works out proposals on their improvement, provides consultations on taxation matters, organization of book-keeping and inner financial control, foreign-trade transactions, operations in foreign currency and the like.

Some control functions are borne by Soviet state bodies (the councils of ministers of Union republics, Gosbank, Vnesheconombank and other concerned ministries and departments), designed to secure the normal performance of JEs in the territory of the USSR.

Joint enterprises are legal entities under Soviet law. As such, the Soviet state grants them various rights and accords them every possible assistance during the initial stages of their activity. The observance of these rights is guaranteed by Decrees 48 and 49 of the USSR Council of Ministers. Therefore the state is bound to exercise control over the proper observance of such rights.

Under adopted legislation JEs are entitled to independent decision-making which should not be contrary to existing legislation. Their activity should not interfere with the normal performance of other enterprises and associations, or aggravate the living conditions of Soviet citizens. In all socialist countries JEs function within the strict observance of the national laws of their host country and within the framework of special provisions stipulating their operation.

Thus state control is designed to ensure cooperation, mutual benefits and equality of all parties to this form of economic activity, based on bona fide principles regarding a foreign partner, and on respect for such partner's interests, and at the same time, to secure the observance of legality and the economic and financial discipline in their economic activity.

According to the USSR Council of Ministers' decree of 12 December 1988, Soviet state enterprises and associations may found JEs or organize international amalgamations together with foreign enterprises and companies provided, they have consent of the respective higher administrative body.

When adopting a decision such administrative bodies verify that the prospective business of the joint enterprise, as elaborated in its constitutive instruments, does not run counter to Soviet law or state interests. The same functions rest with the councils of ministers of Union and autonomous republics and executive committees of regions or other territories which authorize JEs of Soviet production cooperatives and foreign enterprises and companies. When registering a JE the USSR Ministry of Finance also exercises certain control over the completeness and accuracy of its constitutive instruments. (*Editor's note*. As noted above, the registration procedure has changed since the enactment of Decree 49, and registration is no longer carried out at the all-Union level; see Appendix 3.)

Special attention should be given to the financial control over the operation of JEs, exercised primarily by the USSR Ministry of Finance. While effectuating its economic activity, a JE should conduct operative, book-keeping and statistical accounts following the procedure established in the USSR for Soviet state enterprises. Registration and accountability are imperative for the production efficiency of a joint enterprise. Accounts are necessary, first, for a JE itself to have a real financial picture and secure a just distribution of profits. A JE must have accurate information regarding every aspect of its economic activity.

The forms of accounts for JEs are approved by the USSR Ministry of Finance together with the USSR State Committee for Statistics. A JE's book-keeping is carried out following the forms and methods existing in the USSR for Soviet state enterprises. When preparing the basic accounts of its production and financial activity a JE should use typical source documentation established in the USSR for Soviet state enterprises.

The book-keeping and accounting of a JE are carried out by the appropriate personnel headed by a chief accountant who comes under the jurisdiction of the Regulations for Chief Accountants approved by Decree 59 of the USSR Council of Ministers of 24 January 1980.[19]

The chief accountant must secure the accurate accounting of expenses of production and circulation, and of product marketing; the accurate accounting of the results of the enterprise's economic and financial activity; the compilation of accurate book-keeping accounts on the basis of source documents and book-keeping; and submission of management accountancy to appropriate organs within established dates. The chief accountant may not receive for execution and registration documents on operations which are contrary to existing legislation and established procedure for accepting, keeping and spending money resources, commodities and other material valuables.

The book-keeping and statistical accounts of a JE must be submitted in the manner established in the USSR for Soviet state enterprises. For example, Soviet state enterprises are guided by rules of compiling, dates of submitting and procedure for examining and approving book-keeping reports and balances as specified in the Regulations for Book-Keeping Accounts and Balances approved by the Decree of the USSR Council of Ministers of 29 July 1979.[20] Therefore the USSR Ministry of Finance and the USSR State Committee for Statistics are entitled to control the manner and accuracy of accounts at a JE. In the event of non-observance of such rules, a JE is liable under Soviet law (para. 23, Decree 48; para. 45, Decree 49).

The USSR Ministry of Finance is charged with a no less important control function in the field of taxation. Decree 49 specifies that income tax is calculated by a joint enterprise itself, while tax agencies are entitled to verify its accuracy (paras. 37, 38). In case of arrears in payments a pecuniary fine in the amount of 0.005 per cent is charged for each day of delay (para. 39). Collection of overdue taxes is made in the manner provided for foreign juridical persons by the Statute on the Recovery of Tax Payments Not Within the Period, confirmed by the Edict of the Presidium of the USSR Supreme Soviet of 26 January 1981.[21] These matters are settled in greater detail in Instruction 124 on taxation of joint enterprises, adopted by the USSR Ministry of Finance on 4 May 1987. This instruction stipulates *inter alia* that local financial organs are entitled to control the proper estimates and timely and full budgetary payments of income tax, as well as the timely submission of established accounts by taxpayers.

As specified in paragraph 23 of Decree 49, JEs independently work out and approve their economic programmes. Soviet state organizations fix no compulsory planned targets for them and provide no guarantees for marketing their products.

Under current law Gosbank and Vnesheconombank exercise some control functions. The crediting of enterprises comes under direct control of banks. Decrees of the USSR Council of Ministers stipulate that joint enterprises, if it is necessary, may obtain credits on commercial terms: in foreign currency from Vnesheconombank or, with its consent, from foreign banks or other foreign firms; in roubles from Gosbank or Vnesheconombank.

Banking operations and crediting of JEs in Soviet roubles, as well as their maintenance of rouble accounts at USSR banks, are carried out in the same manner as that applicable to Soviet organizations. To obtain credits a borrower submits to Vnesheconombank an application which should specify the purpose of a credit, its sum, the time of repayment, characteristics of the goods or services to be purchased therewith, their cost, the economic effectiveness of using the goods or services and other pertinent factors.

Thus crediting should always be well grounded. Banks are entitled to demand that an applicant account for its financial standing, supply additional data on the designated purposes for the credits, the dates of their repayment and so on. Collateral for the credit might include bills of exchange, guarantees of foreign banks and insurance companies or assets of the JE.

Banks control the designated use, provision and timely repayment of credits granted to a JE. In doing so banking officials regularly conduct documentary check-ups and, where appropriate, undertake field checks. If a credit is not used for its designated purpose a bank may call the credit before its maturity date and terminate the credit agreement.

Where a borrower fails to repay credits on time a bank considers the reasons for late payment and is entitled to effect payment of a borrower's credit obligation by debiting the borrower's current account.

The USSR Ministry of Finance, Gosbank and Vnesheconombank exercise control with respect to the return of a foreign partner's share. Liquidation of a JE is registered with the USSR Ministry of Finance. (*Editor's note.* Insomuch as the registration procedure has changed, so has the procedure regarding liquidation of a JE; see, for example, Appendices 2 and 3.)

In summary, control over the activity of JEs in the USSR is designed to secure legality and the economic and financial discipline necessary to provide beneficial conditions for a joint enterprise's performance.

The efficient functioning of JEs will depend, to a large extent, on proper control over their activity on the part of both their partners and the state organs concerned. The latter, while exercising their respective control functions as specified in existing normative acts, must allow normal performance of JEs and accord them every possible assistance rather than interfere in their production activity.

NOTES

[1]   Decree of the USSR Council of Ministers of 18 December 1980 'On confirmation of the statute of the USSR State Bank', *Sobraniye postanovleniy SSSR*, Art. 112, No. 3, 1981; also para. 6, Decree of the CPSU CC and the USSR Council of Ministers 'On improving the national banking system and enhancing its impact on economic effectiveness', *Sobraniye postanovleniy SSSR*, Art. 121, No. 37, 1987.

[2]   Decree of the USSR Council of Ministers of 7 June 1982 'On confirmation of the statute of the USSR Bank for Foreign Economic Affairs', *Sobraniye postanovleniy SSSR*, Art 95, No. 18, 1982.

[3]   Paragraph 4, Decree of the CPSU CC and the USSR Council of Minsters 'On improving the national banking system . . .'.

[4]   Cf. *inter alia* paras. 3 and 9, 'Regulations for a cost-accounting foreign trade organization (amalgamation)', *Sobraniye postanovleniy SSSR*, Art. 26, No. 6, 1971; Decree of the CPSU CC and the USSR Council of Ministers, 'On measures for improving management of foreign economic contacts', *Sobraniye postanovleniy SSSR*, Art. 172, No. 336, 1986; paras. 2, 8, 25, Decree of 2 December 1988.

[5]   Sections IV and VII of Regulations for Import, Export, Transfer and Overseas Remittances of Soviet and Foreign Currency and Other Currency Valuables, *Sobraniye postanovleniy SSSR*, Art. 65, No. 12, 1982.

[6]   *Vedomosti Verkhovnogo Soveta SSSR*, Art. 712, No. 49, 1976.

[7]   For details see A.B. Altshuler, *International Currency Law* (Moscow, 1984), pp. 81–4 (in Russian).

[8] Decree of the USSR Council of Ministers of 11 November 1982, 'On approving the regulations for bank credits', *Sobraniye postanovleniy SSSR*, Art. 89, No. 13, 1980.

[9] Article 3 of the Law on the State Enterprise (Association) (Moscow, 1987), p. 3 (in Russian).

[10] Edict of the Presidium of the USSR Supreme Soviet of 1 March 1979 'On the income tax levied on cooperatives and social organizations', *Vedomosti Verkhovnogo Soveta SSSR*, Art. 156, No. 10, 1979; Edict of the Presidium of the USSR Supreme Soviet, 'On changes and addenda to the decree on the income tax levied on cooperatives and social organizations', *Vedomosti Verkhovnogo Soveta SSSR*, Art, 90, No. 7, 1987.

[11] Paragraph 32, Decree of 2 December 1988.

[12] Articles 2, 3 and 4 of the Soviet-American Tax Convention, *Vedomosti Verkhovnogo Soveta SSSR*, Art. 177, No. 11, 1976; Articles 5, 6, 7 and 8 of the Convention on Income Taxes, *Vedomosti Verkhovnogo Soveta SSSR*, Art. 1022, No. 50, 1986.

[13] Article 14 of the Convention Between the USSR and Spain on Double Taxation Exemptions on Income and Property, *Vedomosti Verkhovnogo Soveta SSSR*, Art 811, No. 38, 1986.

[14] Article 16 of the Convention Between the USSR and Spain on Double Taxation Exemptions on Income and Property.

[15] *Ekonomicheskaya gazeta*, No. 41, 1987, pp. 18–19.

[16] *Vedomosti Verkhovnogo Soveta SSSR*, Art. 313, No. 20, 1978.

[17] *Vedomosti Verkhovnogo Soveta SSSR*, Art. 122, No. 5, 1981.

[18] Paragraphs 1, 3 and 4 of the Decree of the USSR Council of Ministers and the All-Union Central Council of Trade Unions of 12 September 1983, 'On the procedure for paying dues for the state social insurance', *Sobraniye postanovleniy SSSR*, Art. 149, No. 26, 1983.

[19] *Sobraniye postanovleniy SSSR*, Art. 43, No. 6, 1980.

[20] *Reference Book on Normative Documents for Accountancy*, Vol. 3 (Moscow, 1980), p. 435 (in Russian).

[21] *Vedomosti Verkhovnogo Soveta SSSR*, Art. 122, No. 5, 1981.

1991 SUPPLEMENTARY COMMENTARY

Since the first normative acts on currency and financial aspects of JEs were adopted a host of new legislative acts with a direct relationship with the resolution of these issues was adopted. These included the adoption in 1990 of the Law on the USSR State Bank (Gosbank), the Law on Banks and Bank Activities and the Law on Currency Regulation. In the sphere of taxation a number of corresponding laws were also recently adopted. Foreign banks and banks with the participation of foreign capital may now be created on the territory of the USSR where one of the foreign participants is a bank.

The new legislation on currency regulation recognizes JEs as 'residents' of the USSR. Settlements in foreign economic operations between juridical persons which are residents and juridical persons which are non-residents may be effected in freely convertible currency. A joint enterprise may open a foreign account and carry out operations in connection therewith only upon the permission of Gosbank or the central bank of a republic. A JE may use foreign currency in connection with settlement of accounts in the USSR only in accordance with the procedure established by Soviet legislation on currency regulation.

Joint enteprises enjoy exceptions from the general rules of currency regulation. Unlike regular Soviet enterprises a joint enterprise is not subject to mandatory sales of foreign currency from its foreign currency receipts from foreign economic activity where foreign capital participation in the JE exceeds 30 per cent.

From the perspective of tax regulation JEs in the USSR are divided into two groups: those in which the share of the foreign participant is 30 per cent or less, and those in which such share exceeds 30 per cent. The tax on profits of the first group is established in the measure of 35 per cent. Enterprises in the second group may make use of various tax privileges (a reduction of the tax rate and a tax holiday). In addition, tax privileges are enjoyed by JEs in priority branches of the national economy and in separate regions of the country.

The income of foreign participants resulting from the distribution of profits of the JE are subject to a tax in the measure of 15 per cent upon transfer abroad, if not otherwise provided by an international tax treaty of the USSR. The tax is paid in currency being transferred. Finally legislation also provides for abolition of double taxation of profits or income transferred abroad by foreign participants in a JE.

The foreign investor is guaranteed the transfer abroad of earned profits. In the case of liquidation of a JE, its accumulated assets are subject to taxation at their real value. In the case of liquidation, the investor has the right to compensation of investments due him and revenues received in connection therewith in cash or in kind, according to the real value at the moment of liquidation.

VI

Joint Enterprises and Industrial Property

As noted earlier, Soviet legislation provides for the use in the Soviet economy of advanced foreign technology, the development of the country's export facilities and the reduction of irrational imports. These purposes are among those which underlie the establishment in the Soviet territory of joint enterprises with the participation of firms from foreign nations. This policy presupposes the production by JEs of high quality goods on the basis of higher scientific and technological achievements. It is clear that the realization of these purposes is attended by the use of existing foreign and Soviet technology and by the development of new Soviet equipment. Hence the vast importance of industrial property, in particular the legal protection and use of inventions, for the operation of JEs.

What provisions of Soviet legislation in this sphere are applicable to the activities of JEs? How do they relate to the respective rules of the normative acts on the procedure for the establishment and operation of joint enterprises? How do they correlate with constitutive instruments? And finally, what is the specific nature of the legal protection and use of trade marks as an object of industrial property? Let us consider these questions.

Decree 49 stipulates that the rights to industrial property belonging to joint enterprises are protected in accordance with Soviet legislation, including protection in the form of patents. The procedure for the transfer of the right to industrial property to a joint enterprise by its participants and vice versa, and also the commercial use of such rights and their protection abroad, are determined by the constitutive instruments (para. 17, Decree 49).

Thus Decree 49 refers to Soviet legislation and the JE's constitutive instruments. Despite its laconicism, the relevant paragraph contains a number of important provisions which are of substantial importance for the settlement of the above-mentioned questions. Moreover, the decree provides that the rights to use inventions and know-how may be incorporated alongside other property in the authorized fund of the joint enterprise as contributions.

It follows from the decree that the grounds for the origin of joint enterprises' rights to industrial property include the production of inventions by JEs' employees and the assignment of such rights to the JEs by their participants. This assignment may be effected both during the time the JE is being set up and during its functioning. Moreover, one can regard as a third ground the acquisition of the rights to use inventions from third parties on the basis of appropriate agreements, which joint enterprises may conclude during their economic performance.

What rights arise for joint enterprises when they acquire the right to industrial property on each of these grounds?

In those cases where a foreign participant transfers to the joint enterprise certain inventions protected in the USSR by patents, the question of qualifying the relations between the participant and the joint enterprise is settled unambiguously. In this case the question centres on a licence relation. The foreign participant may also assign its patent rights to the joint enterprise in full. When the right to use an invention is granted by way of a contribution, the constitutive instruments or a special agreement must register both its value and the terms of its use. These documents must also determine whether such a licence is simple or exclusive with regard to Soviet territory and establish how and to what extent the invention in question may be used in the territory of third countries. In both cases (where a licence is granted or patent rights are fully assigned to third parties) it is important to regulate the relations between the joint enterprise's participants concerning these rights in the event the enterprise is liquidated.

The same range of questions must be defined by a foreign participant and a joint enterprise with regard to the inventions protected in the USSR by patents and transferred during the course of the joint enterprise's operation. The difference lies in the fact that the constitutive instruments may fix only some of the general principles of such transfer, while the terms specific to the particular invention must be coordinated by an additional agreement.

Specific questions arise in connection with the transfer by a Soviet participant of inventions protected in the USSR by author's certificates, regarding such participant's contributions during both the foundation of the respective joint enterprise and its operation thereafter. According to the 1973 Statute on Discoveries, Inventions and Innovative Proposals, the author's certificate gives legislative recognition to the exclusive right of the Soviet state to inventions, while granting personal proprietary and non-proprietary rights to the inventors themselves. Enterprises and organizations in which inventions have been created and which are participants in joint enterprises do not acquire any rights on the basis of their author's certificates. Rather, in the cases under review the joint enterprise is granted a licence to make use of industrial property belonging to the state (readers will note that this is not only an act of *use* but also an act of *disposition of rights*). Thus the Soviet participant must receive the corresponding permission from competent Soviet bodies for the assignment of these rights. In other words, the question arises as to how relations between Soviet participants in joint enterprises and the state are regulated in connection with the said assignments. (*Editor's note*. The 1973 Statute was replaced by the USSR Law on Inventions of 1991.)

In light of current legislation the settlement of this question depends largely on the qualification of the relations between the joint enterprise and its participants. If rights to industrial property are assigned as a *contribution* to the authorized fund, the assignment is regulated either by the foundation agreement or a special agreement between the participants in the joint enterprise, either of which will constitute a foreign economic agreement. Under paragraph 1 of Decree 1078 of the USSR Council of Ministers of 12 December 1978,[1] if an agreement which is concluded in the sphere of international economic, scientific and technological cooperation provides for the legal protection and use of joint and Soviet inventions in a country which does not possess the right to these inventions, then the terms thereof must be approved by the USSR State Committee for Inventions and Discoveries.[2] (*Editor's note*. With the passage of the 1991 Law on Inventions, the State Committee for Inventions and Discoveries has been replaced by the State Patent Office, or Gospatent.)

Because the right to industrial property assigned as a contribution from a Soviet participant may be used by a joint enterprise not only in Soviet territory but also abroad (for example in the export of goods), then the terms of any foundation or special agreement must be agreed upon in the statutory manner with the USSR State Committee for

Inventions and Discoveries. It would be superfluous for a joint enterprise to receive any other special permission for a licence.

What procedure should apply to the transfer of technology between Soviet organizations and JEs?

The answer to this question depends on whether the agreements between Soviet organizations and JEs are recognized as domestic transactions or as foreign-trade transactions. Initially, such agreements were qualified as domestic by way of interpretation. More recently, however, the qualification was recorded in Soviet legislation (as in the Statute on Deliveries of Technical Products): the agreements are now regarded as domestic transactions, to which general norms of civil and special economic legislation are applicable. Consequently, the authorization procedure for the sale and purchase of licences applicable to foreign-trade transactions should not apply to the transfer of technology between Soviet organizations and joint enterprises.

The assignment by a foreign participant of the rights to the use of an invention protected in the USSR by an author's certificate also has certain specific features. Soviet jurists previously considered that, with regard to cooperation between organizations of socialist countries, the concept of the licensing agreement, in cases where the right to the use of an invention is protected in the licencee's country by an author's certificate, does not correspond to the classical concept of the licensing agreement as authorization on the use of the protected rights.[3]

The gist of this agreement consists not in granting the right to the use of an invention,[4] but in making possible the real use of the invention, which fact necessitates the transfer of the author's know-how.

Nevertheless, it is possible to state that in the aforementioned cases the matter concerns the transfer of one's own scientific and technical results, the rights to which belong either to the participant in the JE or to its state, depending on the form of legal protection. In this context we regard as inexact the provision in Decree 49 that the procedure for the transfer of rights to industrial property to a JE by its participants or by the JE to its participants (and also the procedure for the commercial use of these rights and their protection abroad) is determined by the constitutive instruments.

The foundation agreement regulates the procedure for the establishment and operation of a JE and the relations between the JE and its participants. It must therefore contain provisions on mutual relations regarding the assignment of rights to industrial property. But the procedure for legal protection and for the use of one's own results belonging to the participants in the JE is regulated above all by the norms of the national legislation of the participant's country.

Furthermore, these questions may be regulated by contracts concluded with third persons especially when a participant in the JE has created an invention which it transfers in the course of scientific and technical work under the contract of cooperation or order concluded with a third person.

As was noted above, the second ground for a JE's acquisition of rights to inventions is the development of inventions by the employees of the JE during the course of its operation. In such case the question arises: to whom do the rights to such results belong? In settling this question, of great importance in our view is the form of the newly created enterprise. In other words, it is significant whether it is an independent JE or an international economic amalgamation created on the principles of preserving national ownership of the participants' chattels with the purpose of carrying on coordination activity.

With regard to joint enterprises and organizations carrying on their own economic activity two approaches are possible in principle: (*a*) inventions made at JEs are the joint inventions of their participants; or (*b*) such inventions belong to the JE as an independent subject of law.

Before considering each of these approaches we ought to dwell on the current international concepts of the right to a joint scientific and technical result in general and to a joint invention in particular, since there is a distinction between them. The legal treatment of an unprotected scientific and technical result is specified exclusively by the agreement between the participating parties. On the other hand, the legal treatment of an invention is specified, on the one hand, by the terms of the agreement on cooperation (regardless of the type of agreement) and, on the other hand, by the norms of national legislation of the state (or states) in which protection is provided, which norms depend on the form of legal protection.

International documents which in one way or another concern questions on the creation, protection and use of inventions in economic, scientific and technological cooperation[5] (despite the differences in the criteria of referring inventions to the category of joint individual results) coincide in determining the scope of rights to joint inventions. Such rights include (*a*) the right to legal protection in the countries of the participating parties; (*b*) the right to legal protection in third countries; (*c*) the right to the use of inventions in the countries of the participating parties; and (*d*) the right to the use of inventions in third countries, including the export of goods produced with the application of a joint invention. Thus the concept 'the right to a joint invention' includes the right to joint legal protection and the right to the joint use of the invention. Therefore the parties possess the full right to a joint invention in the strict sense of the word only when their rights are based on the mutually received protective documents. If the protective documents are issued in behalf of the cooperating party, the rights of the other party become restricted to some extent and are based on the agreement. In terms of patent legislation such invention will not be regarded as joint, because only one subject is the bearer of legally protected rights.

If we adopt the point of view that inventions made at a JE are collective inventions in the above-mentioned sense, this will mean that protective documents and the ensuing rights belong not to the JE but to its participants. Although such decision is possible in principle through an agreement between the founders, in our view this essentially restricts the independence of the JE in the exercise of its economic functions, which runs counter to the principles of 'full economic accountability, non-subsidy and self-financing' in their operation (see para. 6, Decree 49). Moreover, this kind of decision will complicate the process of receiving legal protection for such inventions.

This approach to the problem contradicts the above-mentioned provisions of Decree 49 which deal with the rights to industrial property belonging to the JE and with the transfer of these rights by the JE to its participants. Therefore the most correct approach is the second one, which recognizes that the rights to inventions made at a JE belong to the JE itself, which is an independent Soviet legal person, and not to its participants. This approach corresponds to international practice.

In the light of the foregoing we must consider whether the recognition of a JE's rights to inventions contradicts paragraph 26b of Article 2 of the 'Agreement on the legal protection of inventions, generally useful industrial designs and trade marks in economic, scientific and technological cooperation', executed on 12 April 1973. This agreement states: 'Inventions, generally useful industrial designs created in international research institutes, development establishments, joint laboratories and departments, international organizations and collectives are joint, regardless of the fact whether these inventions, industrial and generally useful designs were created by nationals of one country or several countries parties to the agreement, unless agreements on the formation of such organizations and collectives provide otherwise. The rights to such inventions, industrial and generally useful designs belong to the countries – members of the said organization, collectives – or to the relevant organizations of these countries, since this practice is allowed by national legislation.'

Thus the agreement of 12 April 1973 vests the right to industrial property not in an international organization but in its participants. At first glance we have here a discrepancy between the provisions of the agreement and the norms of Soviet legislation. However, we underscore the fact that this agreement deals with organizations whose participants are CMEA member countries and not their economic organizations. The agreement is oriented toward international organizations, which as a rule are not engaged in economic activity, since at the time of its conclusion the creation of international economic organizations (for example joint enterprises) was not a widely-used form of cooperation.

The conclusion that the agreement of 12 April 1973 was not intended for cooperation in the form of JEs is confirmed by the fact that after it was signed by the CMEA member countries a number of agreements were concluded to set up international economic amalgamations, whose statutes provided that the amalgamation and its affiliates have the right on their behalf to possess, use and dispose of its property and also acquire and exercise other proprietary rights, including those to non-material objects (that is rights to industrial property).

In the light of the foregoing it appears more appropriate to apply to a JE the concept of the JE's *own* inventions and not the concept of joint inventions, which presupposes several subjects possessing the rights to them, since the JE as such and not its participants collectively is the bearer of legally protected rights.

It is a different matter that the procedure for the realization of the JE's rights must be jointly determined in constitutive instruments by all participants. In any case, decision-making on the legal protection and use of inventions in most cases will be practised by the governing bodies of the JE which is composed of representatives of its participants.

However, from a legal point of view, such governing bodies represent not the participants of the JE but *the enterprise as an independent subject of Soviet law*, which itself decides the fate of each concrete invention, including the terms of its transfer to the participants. The settlement of this question in a given instance may be different. Two options are possible: the gratuitous transfer by a JE of its inventions to its participants, or the transfer thereof by the JE to the participants for consideration. First, this may be dictated by the need to give effect to the principles of economic accountability, non-subsidy and self-financing in the JE's operation. Second, in cases where inventions are made by the JE through the implementation of contracts with third persons (by way of cooperation, orders, etc.), the terms of their transfer to the JE's participants will be determined by the terms of such contracts.

In any case, questions involved in the legal protection and use of inventions must be reflected in constitutive instruments. We will note in this connection that so far these questions have not been regulated in detail in constitutive instruments. Most of these documents merely repeat the applicable paragraphs of Decree 49.

At the same time an analysis of some terms of the constitutive instruments and agreements shows that they proceed from the recognition that rights to objects of industrial property created at the joint enterprise belong to the JE, and that the transfer thereof by the JE to its participants is made, as a rule, on a compensatory basis under individual contracts, or the terms of such transfer are determined by the board on an ad hoc basis.

It stands to reason that it is quite difficult to regulate in detail the legal protection and use of industrial property in constitutive instruments because they contain a wide range of questions. Therefore in certain cases it is advisable to conclude special agreements on these questions in the form of supplements to the constitutive instruments.

The question of who possesses the rights to inventions made within the framework of international economic amalgamations established to coordinate the economic activity of their participants is settled on the principle of the national ownership of their chattels, when the enterprises which are part of such amalgamations do not lose the qualities of an independent subject of law of the country's location.

In such cases inventions made at enterprises which are part of the amalgamation, carry on their own economic activity, act as legal persons under national law and deal with the protection of industrial property must be subject to the law of the country's location. As a rule relations between them are based on contracts. The authors of inventions enter into labour relations with such enterprises and not with the amalgamation itself, a fact of essential importance for the determination of the procedure for the legal protection and use of so-called official inventions.

It appears that such circumstances are responsible for the principal variant in which the rights to inventions made at the enterprises forming the amalgamation belong to these enterprises, for in the final analysis the acquisition of such rights is not an end in itself but the purpose of their exercise in the territory of the patenting country, that is of the economic activity in one form or another. As for amalgamations established solely to discharge coordination functions, they do not carry on such activities.

If a joint organization is set up to carry on research and development for the benefit of its participants on the basis of common property, as paragraph 2 of Decree 48 provides, the rights ensuing from the protective documents are enjoyed by this organization or the amalgamation as such, which fact must be settled in constitutive instruments or in a special document on industrial property. A special procedure for the use of relevant inventions by agreement among the amalgamation's participants will be introduced here as in the case of a JE, but the legally protected rights to industrial property will be enjoyed by the one subject.

In the Soviet Union we have dealt in detail on this question, given its practical importance. The question determines who actually will have rights and obligations in regarding industrial property, in what manner rights will be exercised both in the Soviet territory and abroad, and which rules of Soviet legislation on the legal protection of inventions are applicable to joint enterprises. Let us analyze these questions in the light of the above-stated position.

First, let us consider the form of legal protection, as it is a second factor which determines the legal treatment of inventions. Under Decrees 48 and 49 the rights to industrial property belonging to joint enterprises, international amalgamations and organizations are protected by Soviet law, including protection in the form of patents. The patent is not the only form of protection. Protection may also be extended in the form of an author's certificate. However, analysis of the rules of USSR special legislation warrants the conclusion that inventions created at JEs may not be protected in the form of the author's certificate.

Under paragraph 27 of the Statute on Discoveries, Inventions and

Innovative Proposals of 1973, inventions protected by author's certificates may be used by Soviet state-owned, cooperative and social enterprises, organizations and institutions proceeding from the interests of the state and these organizations, and in the absence of a special permission. Such inventions may be used by other organizations and persons with the purpose of carrying on a relevant trade within 15 years after the day the application was made for an invention, but only with the authorization of the USSR State Committee for Inventions and Discoveries. (*Editor's note*. As indicated above, as of 1 July 1991 only patents, not authors' certificates, are granted in the USSR.)

As a JE does not meet the above standards (because it is not a state, cooperative or social organization), protection in the form of the author's certificate is of no meaning to it, as it cannot use its own invention without a special authorization. Consequently the procedure for the legal protection of inventions created at JEs will be determined in practice by the rules concerning protection in the form of a patent. The question of safeguarding the rights of a joint enterprise to inventions created by its employees in the course of their employment must be settled by the JE's constitutive instruments and by employment agreements with these employees.

Under the 1973 statute the question of paying remuneration to the authors of inventions must be settled in the same manner, as the rules of Soviet law on authors' fees for inventions made in the course of employment are applicable to inventions protected in the USSR by an author's certificate, not by the patent.

A JE's constitutive instruments may provide that in all countries wherever it is possible applications will be made by the respective JE. If the national legislation of the patenting country allows for the application by the author alone the inventor must reassign the rights ensuing from him to the JE, which in turn must guarantee the inventor the payment of the author's fees.

Regarding the Soviet Union, this will mean that the application will be made on behalf of the JE which is the successor to the author, and the fact of succession will require certification by appropriate documentation. In the future, however, it would be advisable to introduce pertinent provisions into Soviet legislation.

Regarding legal protection of inventions created in a JE abroad, Decree 49 envisages that the procedure for this will be determined by the JE's constitutive instruments.

In addition to the legal protection and use of inventions for JEs, of great importance are the questions involved in the use of trade marks. The participants in a JE must above all decide whether they will use the trade mark belonging to one of them and intended for the designation of goods produced at the JE or whether they will create a special trade mark. This decision in any given instance will depend on any number of factors, including the nature of the goods the JE will produce, the possession by one or more participants of their own trade marks and the reputation of such marks in the target markets.

The constitutive instruments of JEs registered to date evidence use of both variants. At the same time, an analysis of these documents shows that they regulate the use of trade marks with varying degrees of elaboration. Some instruments contain special articles that regulate the matter in detail, while others make only brief reference to the designation of the JE's goods by a trade mark.

It is characteristic that relations concerning a JE's use of a trade mark are spelled out in greatest detail in those cases where the JE is granted the right to use the mark of one of its participants. For example, the charter of one JE (whose participants are a Soviet amalgamation and a Finnish firm) regulates in detail the relations connected with the use by the JE of the firm's trade mark. Under the charter the firm granted the JE a simple gratuitous licence on the use of its trade mark in Soviet territory for the duration of the firm's participation in the JE. The charter stipulates that the firm and the JE will come to terms on a case-by-case basis regarding the JE's use of the trade mark outside the USSR. The JE may not, without the firm's written consent, reassign its right to use the trade mark in Soviet territory to third persons.

By and large the above-mentioned provisions of the charter in question reflect the range of issues which must be regulated during the transfer of rights to use a participant's trade mark: the type of licence, the territory in which rights may be exercised, the financial conditions and the period of a licence's validity. Constitutive documents may also specify liability for breach and quality guarantees for goods designated by the mark. The obligation to register a trade mark in the USSR and to maintain it in force should also be addressed.

As distinct from the foregoing, those constitutive instruments which envisage the creation of a special trade mark for a JE's goods seldom contain detailed conditions for the legal protection and use of the mark. These documents often merely recite the fact that the JE has (or will have) one or more trade marks subject to registration in the USSR.

At the same time certain issues concerning such marks must be regulated. For example, in whose name will the trade mark be registered in the USSR and abroad? Who bears the obligations to register it and to maintain the registration?

The specifics of the national legislation of various countries in this sphere must be taken into account. It must be determined in accordance with the decision of the above issues who (and on what conditions) has the right to use and dispose of the trade mark, and what happens if the JE ceases to operate, or if one of its participants withdraws or is replaced.

(*Editor's note.* Readers should note that registration of trade marks and service marks by joint enterprises in the USSR is now effectuated in accordance with the USSR Law on Trade Marks and Service Marks, adopted in 1991.)

In conclusion, it should be emphasized that the creation of joint enterprises in the Soviet Union as a new form of international economic cooperation has naturally given rise to a number of questions which earlier were not regulated by legislation in the sphere of the legal protection and use of rights to industrial property. Therefore we are faced with the tasks of improving this legislation in order to make it conform with the requirements of modern international economic relations and of regulating in greater detail the questions of industrial property in constitutive instruments and special agreements.

NOTES

[1]   *Sobraniye postanovleniy SSSR*, Art. 17, No. 4, 1979.

[2]   In 1987 this Committee was transformed into a State Committee under the USSR State Committee for Science and Technology.

[3]   *International Transfer of Technology: Legal Regulation* (Moscow, 1985), p. 48 (in Russian).

[4]   In this particular case no authorization is required, since the exclusive rights belong to the state of the recipient side.

[5]   These documents include (i) the 'Agreement on the legal protection of inventions, generally useful industrial designs and trade marks in economic, scientific and technological cooperation' of 12 April 1973, concluded by CMEA member countries (see *Soviet Legislation on Inventions*, 2nd ed. (Moscow, 1983), pp. 174–84, in Russian); (ii) the 'Agreement between the government of the USSR and the government of the French Republic on the mutual protection and use of rights to industrial property' of 19 May 1970 (see *Collected Treaties, Agreements and*

Conventions Concluded by the USSR with Foreign States, Issue XXVI (Moscow, 1973), pp. 103–4, in Russian); (iii) the 'Agreement between the government of the USSR and the government of Austria on the legal protection of industrial property' of 10 April 1981 (see *Collected International Treaties and Agreements of the USSR,* Issue 38 (Moscow, 1984), pp. 104–7, in Russian).

1991 SUPPLEMENTARY COMMENTARY

In 1991 the Soviet Union adopted a number of new laws in the sphere of industrial property. These included the Law on Inventions in the USSR, the Fundamental Principles of Civil Legislation of the USSR and the Republics, and the Law on Trade Marks and Service Marks in the USSR.

The adoption of these laws has great significance for the regulation of relations arising out of the creation and use of inventions and other objects of industrial property by JEs and other enterprises with foreign investment. In particular we should note the demise of the inventor's certificate as the basic form of protection of inventions and in its place a move to the patent as the sole means of such protection.

The Law on Inventions and the Fundamental Principles effectively combine to create a single, unified patent system in the USSR. Henceforth all inventions are to be protected by patents issued by one all-Union organ, the USSR State Patent Office (Gospatent). Such patents are to be effective over the entire territory of the USSR and are valid for 20 years from the submission of the respective patent application to Gospatent. Under previous law a patent was valid for only 15 years. The patent holder has the *exclusive*, inalienable right to use the invention. No person may use a patented invention without the permission of the patent holder.

Any 'introduction into economic turnover' (that is manufacture, application, import, offer or sale) of a product containing a patented invention, or the application of any process protected by a patent, is deemed to be an infringement of the patent holder's rights. The law establishes property liability for patent infringement. Upon the demand of a patent holder an infringement must be terminated and compensation must be paid for losses incurred as a result of the infringement.

The Law on Inventions contains special rules concerning enterprises with foreign investment. As a general rule the law applies to such enterprises. However, two exceptions to this rule are provided. The first concerns the treatment of employees' inventions, and the second concerns patenting abroad. Regarding employees' inventions the law provides that the provisions of an agreement concluded between an employee and an enterprise with foreign investment shall be applied except as otherwise provided in the enterprise's foundation documents. Thus such enterprises may establish their own ground rules on how employee inventions are treated. As an example: a joint stock society organized under new Soviet joint stock society legislation, which is wholly owned by a Delaware corporation, may provide in its charter that all employment contracts concluded with Soviet employees shall include provisions on inventions created by such employees during their employment, and such provisions shall be substantially similar to those applicable to inventions created by employees of its parent corporation in the United States.

As regards patenting abroad (that is in countries other than the USSR) of inventions created in the USSR by employees of an enterprise with foreign investment, the enterprise independently has the right to decide whether to obtain a foreign patent. The law's general rule that an enterprise must first notify Gospatent of its intention to patent an invention abroad does not apply. However, such enterprise must satisfy one condition: before submission of the patent application for an invention in a foreign country an application must be submitted in the USSR.

In connection with the creation of JEs using technology or trade marks of one of the partners, the practice of concluding ancillary agreements on confidentiality of information and trade mark licensing gained great significance. The Fundamental Principles of Civil Legislation also introduced protection of production secrets, including know-how, which will have great significance in the conclusion of agreements on the creation of joint enterprises.

VII

Regulation of Labour at Joint Enterprises

Labour management and its regulation is a crucial issue which arises during the course of a JE's operation. It involves a number of problems, some of which have already been resolved, while many others are yet to be addressed. This is largely due to the fact that the operation of JEs in the territory of the USSR is a phenomenon rather new for the Soviet economy. In passing relevant legal acts law-makers must look into the future – employing mainly prognostic analysis rather than established practice and acquired experience.

Specific features of labour regulation of JEs are the function of the so-called 'foreign element' present both at the level of labour management (management is comprised of Soviet and foreign citizens) and employment (although personnel is mostly Soviet, employment of foreigners is not ruled out). This element poses a question of the relationship between the general regulation of labour at JEs, applicable to both Soviet and foreign employees, and the specific regulation of certain issues related to the presence of the 'foreign element' at these JEs.

According to paragraph 1 of Decree 49, joint enterprises' activities are governed by Soviet law, subject to the exemptions provided by international agreements of the USSR. The regulation of labour applicable to JEs is not specifically exempted from this rule. Furthermore, the national legal regime regulating labour relations in the USSR is extended to Soviet citizens at joint enterprises.

Article 1 of the Fundamental Principles of Labour Legislation of the USSR and Union republics states that 'Soviet legislation on labour regulates labour relations of all workers and employees'. As to the exemptions from the national legal regime allowed for under Decree 49, Soviet labour legislation contains a very important provision guaranteeing that exemptions may only broaden and in no way curtail the rights of the working people in relation to existing legislation.

Article 5 of the Fundamental Principles of Labour Legislation stipulates that 'provisions of labour agreements worsening the situation of workers and employees in relation to the legislation on labour of the USSR and Union republics are invalid'. Not only provisions of labour agreements but also provisions of any other agreements establishing labour conditions for specific employees or work collectives fall into the category of labour agreements whose provisions can be found invalid.[1] However, there would be no reason to apply this provision to international agreements if they set forth exemptions from Soviet legislation.

Under Soviet legislation the national legal regime of the USSR extends to foreigners working in Soviet territory. According to Article 7 of the Law on the Legal Status of Foreign Citizens in the USSR, foreign citizens permanently residing in the USSR may be employed at enterprises, institutions and organizations or be engaged in other labour activity on terms and in accord with procedures established for Soviet citizens. Foreign citizens temporarily residing in the USSR may be involved in labour activity if it is compatible with the purpose for their stay in the USSR.[2]

The legal regime of labour of foreign citizens in the USSR depends to a great extent on their partners in labour relations – Soviet enterprises, foreign firms or international organizations, or, on the other hand, on relevant international bilateral or multilateral agreements. If a foreign citizen concludes an agreement with a Soviet enterprise (when a relevant international agreement does not exist), his work will be regulated by Soviet legislation. If foreign firms send their foreign employees to work in the USSR on the basis of an appropriate international agreement, such employees' work will be subject to both Soviet and foreign national legislation, as well as provisions of pertinent international agreements. In addition a legal relationship is established between them and the enterprise (organization) in the USSR to which they are assigned, to the extent that Soviet labour legislation or relevant international agreements apply to them. At the same time foreign citizens maintain their working relations with the firm which sent them, since they have not terminated their work agreements with such firm. A third alternative is also possible. When an international organization (or its affiliate or division) operating in Soviet territory signs a work agreement with an employee the working conditions of the employee are determined, as a rule, by the international organization itself.

Legal regulation of labour with the so-called 'foreign element' has already been put into practice in the USSR, and a certain amount of experience (albeit not great) has been accumulated. A certain approach to legal regulation of labour has been developed. It can be basically described as a combination of the unity and differentiation of labour conditions which are determined by a number of factors, ranging from the degree of public ownership of the production base to the composition of personnel at an enterprise, institution or organization. At present it is already possible to identify certain specific aspects of regulation: (*a*) variety of legal sources (national and international) and their combination; (*b*) precedence of the Soviet national legal regime except in cases regulated by corresponding international agreements or constitutive instruments; (*c*) due regard for specific features determined by the presence of the 'foreign element' in the sphere of labour by means of reference to the legislation of the country of citizenship. Extension of the national regime of legal regulation of labour to enterprises, institutions and organizations operating in the territory of the USSR ensures their optimal 'adaptation' to the 'social environment', that is the legal system operating in given specific conditions. In its turn this factor becomes one of the most important conditions for the efficient functioning of these enterprises, institutions and organizations. Furthermore, differentiation of legal regulation of labour makes it possible to take into consideration as much as possible the 'foreign element' by establishing exemptions from the national regime.

Legal regulation of labour at joint enterprises has, like legal regulation in general, its object and subjects, sources and methods.

Labour relations (including with respect to both Soviet and foreign citizens) emerging in the process of joint production at such enterprises become the *object* of regulation.

Labour relations at a JE comprise both *individual* and *collective* labour relations. These in turn interact closely and actively with each other. An individual employee and a JE (through its management) are participants in the first type of relations, whereas the labour collective (through its trade-union organization) and the JE (through its management) are participants the latter type. Consequently the employee, the labour collective (trade-union organization) and JE (management) act as *subjects* of labour relations at joint enterprises. It is typical of JEs that a 'foreign element' may be present in each of the subjects of labour relations.

However, the extent of the presence of such 'foreign element' at a particular JE may vary depending on the distribution of the shares among its participants, the nature and conditions of its activities and the purposes and objectives it pursues. In its turn this factor cannot influence the application of the Soviet national legal regime to the activities of the JE and the exemptions from such regime, including legal regulation of labour relations.

An analysis of the first joint enterprises established in the USSR shows that the proportion of foreign specialists in the personnel of such enterprises may considerably decrease and reach some 2 per cent of the total manpower strength from the time of their establishment to the stage of their full development. For instance, an agreement on the establishment of one joint enterprise stipulated that the personnel was to be manned mainly by Soviet citizens and comprise 220 workers and 40 specialists and employees. Of the latter, 24 were to be Soviet citizens, and 16 were to be foreigners. Furthermore, it was envisaged that after the enterprise became fully operational the number of foreign specialists could be reduced to 3–5 persons.

It is well known that the specific features of the object of legal regulation determine to a large extent its *method*. Extension of the national legal regime of the USSR to regulation of labour relations within the framework of joint enterprises presupposes the use of a corresponding method as well.

As regards Soviet labour legislation the method of regulation is characterized by the following distinctive features: (*a*) combination of centralized and local regulation[3]; (*b*) broad participation of workers, their trade-union organizations and labour collectives in the management of enterprises; (*c*) establishment of certain labour conditions directly by the parties to a specific individual labour relationship, namely the employee and the enterprise (for instance, amount of wages, place of work and labour function, that is trade, qualification and post).

Such an approach appears to be quite rational and logical. The point is that the law as regulator of public relations is called upon to combine and harmonize the interests of participants and the interests of society as a whole. It is centralized regulation that is called upon to reflect and take into account the latter circumstance. Local regulation expresses the interests of enterprises as legally independent participants in economic turnover. The interests of the workers and their work collectives are realized through trade unions and labour collectives which participate in the adoption and implementation of decisions at the level of individual enterprises. Finally, the interests of each individual employee are reflected in the conditions of labour which are established in individual labour contracts between the employee and the management of the enterprise.

With regard to joint enterprises it is possible and necessary to speak of specific adaptation of the method of legal regulation of labour relations by Soviet law to the specific features of the object of regulation whose essential feature, as was mentioned above, is the presence of the 'foreign element'. Thus at the level of centralized regulation specific features of the method manifest themselves in that exemptions from the national legal regime applicable to the activities of joint enterprises may be provided for by such 'centralized' (from the perspective of labour law) international legal acts as international treaties of the USSR.

The 'foreign element' at the local level manifests itself in that the content of the collective agreement which management of the joint enterprise must conclude with the trade-union organization, including provisions concerning social development of the collective, is determined by Soviet legislation and the constitutive documents. Thus it appears that the JE's constitutive documents can also be considered as 'local' legal acts from the perspective of labour law.

However, this does not exhaust the list of legal documents which can be worked out and adopted at a joint enterprise, because it will be necessary to take into consideration the 'foreign element' in view of the problems concerning the routine of work and leisure, labour discipline, material incentives and the like. Experience demonstrates that adoption and elaboration of such documents are provided for in the constitutive documents of joint enterprises. For instance, the statute of one joint enterprise mentions such local acts as staff rules and rules of internal labour procedures.

At the level of the individual labour relationship the 'foreign element' is taken into account by providing the possibility to establish certain conditions of work on the basis of an agreement between the management of a joint enterprise and a foreign citizen (see, for example, para. 48, Decree 49).

What is the correlation between these three levels? What aspects of legal regulation of labour at joint enterprises are resolved at centralized and local levels and what issues are settled in specific individual labour agreements?

Before answering these questions, the author would like to touch upon the *sources* of legal regulation of labour at joint enterprises. It is possible to include into this category, first, the entire system of centralized legislative and other legal acts of the USSR having relation to labour regulation as well as corresponding international treaties which establish exemptions from such acts; second, local standard acts, the most important of which are the collective agreement and constitutive documents of a joint enterprise; third, individual labour contracts concluded by the management of joint enterprises both with Soviet and foreign citizens. It is precisely those legal sources that set standards to solve the issue concerning the correlation between centralized, local and individual regulation of labour at joint enterprises.

Section VI of Decree 49, entitled 'Personnel of joint enterprises', mentions the collective agreement, whose content is determined by Soviet legislation and the constitutive documents, as the first among the acts regulating labour relations. In accordance with Article 7 of the Fundamental Principles of Labour Legislation the collective agreement shall contain the main provisions concerning labour and wages established for the given enterprise in accordance with existing legislation as well as provisions relating to work periods, leisure, salary and material incentives and labour protection, which are elaborated by the management and the trade union of the venture within the scope of the rights given to them and which have a standard-setting nature.

Consequently the first case deals with a reproduction of standards set on a centralized basis in the collective agreement, while the second applies to standards of a local nature established at the level of the enterprise. The latter includes, for instance, provisions establishing systems of payment for certain groups of workers, lists of trades and jobs paid for in accordance with rates established for employees employed at peak production areas and in difficult jobs, jobs with harmful and particularly difficult job conditions; lists of jobs and trades giving the employees the right to receive milk or other equivalent food products due to harmful conditions of work; lists of jobs and trades giving the employees the right to receive free work clothes, footwear and other means of individual protection; lists of employees working unregulated working hours, specifying the length of additional leave for each job; lists of jobs on which it is impossible to establish, due to production conditions, a break for rest and eating, and some others.

Thus remaining problems of legal regulation are solved on the basis of the rules of Soviet legislation and the JE's constitutive documents. As regards the former, they apparently include the rules contained in both main legislative acts dealing with labour regulation in the USSR (for instance, the Fundamental Principles of Labour Legislation of the USSR, legal codes on labour of the Union republics, edicts of the Presidium of the USSR Supreme Soviet and Union republics, decrees of the USSR Council of Ministers, etc.) and special legal documents regulating activities of joint ventures (for example Decree 49). In this connection one cannot but mention that a combination of general and special legal acts seems to be the most appropriate method, as it ensures a rather flexible incorporation of the 'foreign element' at the level of centrally regulated labour at joint enterprises.

As regards constitutive instruments (which in addition to Soviet legislation determine the content of the collective agreement at joint enterprises), it has already been mentioned that they should be placed in the category of acts established at the local level. In this connection a question arises concerning the correlation between local acts and centralized acts. There is no doubt that the latter take precedence over the former in the hierarchy of legal acts. This circumstance under Soviet legal doctrine means that both the statute and the agreement on the establishment of a joint enterprise operate *only* when they do not run counter to superior (in this case centralized) acts.

Therefore it is possible to state that constitutive documents as legal acts determining the content of collective agreements at joint enterprises have a *secondary* nature in relation to the rules of Soviet legislation which are incorporated in these agreements. This is emphasized by paragraph 7 of Decree 49, which stipulates that in addition to the provisions spelled out in the decree the statute of a joint enterprise may include other provisions which do not run counter to Soviet legislation and deal with the specific aspects of the enterprise's activity. It should be noted that this provision is just an example demonstrating how a centralized legal act determines the scope of operation and limits of regulation by the local act (statute) of the specific aspects of a joint enterprise's activities. Apart from this, constitutive documents may also be considered as those labour contracts which under Article 5 of the Fundamental Principles of Labour Legislation are recognized as null and void if they worsen conditions of the employees as compared to the existing legislation or otherwise run counter to this legislation.

Thus the collective agreement is one of the main local legal acts establishing conditions of work at joint enterprises. It is possible to incorporate the 'foreign element' into the content of this document with the help of constitutive documents in addition to the Soviet legislation. This possibility is also available from the point of view of subject composition of labour relations regulated by the collective agreement. For instance, in accordance with Article 6 of the Fundamental Principles of Labour Legislation, the collective agreement covers all the employees of an enterprise regardless of whether they are trade union members. Consequently terms of the collective agreement concluded by the management of a joint enterprise and the trade-union organization established at it *also* cover the foreign citizens who work at the enterprise, regardless of their membership in the trade-union organization which signed the agreement.

Further on, Section VI of Decree 49 deals with common features and differences in legal regulation of labour of Soviet and foreign citizens working at joint enterprises. Rules of Soviet legislation concerning the routine of work and leisure (except leaves) and social security equally apply to both. Different approaches are used with respect to wages, leaves and pensions. Rules of Soviet legislation apply to Soviet citizens. However, it does not mean that legal regulation of labour concerning such issues at joint enterprises for Soviet citizens should be absolutely identical to legal regulation of labour at Soviet enterprises. Naturally, when necessary, law-makers have the right to adopt decisions taking into account specific conditions of work of Soviet citizens at joint enterprises.

As regards foreigners, individual legal regulation is applied to them – that is such issues are resolved in a contract signed with each foreign citizen individually. In other words it represents an exemption from the national legal regime of labour for foreign citizens.

What is the nature of such exemption, and how can it be explained? Generally speaking, what is the criterion separating the general and the particular in legal regulation of labour of Soviet and foreign citizens at ventures of this kind? Does it exist at all?

Answers to these questions pertain to the socio-economic sphere rather than to the legal one. First, general legal regulation in this case is determined by the supremacy of national legal regulation of labour in the USSR which, in its turn, is based on the fact that the personnel of joint enterprises on the one hand is mainly comprised of Soviet citizens and on the other that the level of labour rights for Soviet citizens working at joint enterprises should not be less than for employees of Soviet enterprises. This is a manifestation of one of the most essential principles of socialism – the principle of social justice.

However, a question may arise whether the level of labour rights at joint enterprises can be higher than at Soviet enterprises, for instance, in the areas of wages, work and leisure regimes, social security and social insurance.

When answering such questions it is necessary to state first that Soviet labour legislation, while ensuring on the one hand uniform regulation of labour conditions, thereby guarantees a minimum of rights (both in quantity and in scope) of employees and equality of their opportunities in the sphere of labour. On the other hand rules of Soviet labour legislation which are based on objective criteria – such as, for instance, climatic conditions, degree of importance of an industry for society, occupation; complexity, harmfulness and hazardous nature of production process; quantity and quality of labour input of the employees (their work collectives) – establish varying levels of labour conditions. In other words, they carry out their differentiation and ensure through this actual equality of the working people.

Combination of unity and differentiation in legal regulation of labour in the USSR is closely linked to the main principle of socialism – 'From each according to his abilities, to each according to his work'. By acting as a legal mechanism regulating the measure of labour and consumption the labour law is called upon to take into consideration varying conditions of labour, varying qualification of the workers, territorial location of enterprises and other criteria in order to ensure equal pay for equal work.

In doing so differentiation of labour is carried out both at centralized and local levels of regulation of labour relations. In the latter case a superior legal act (that is centralized act) establishes for a specific local act only the minimum or both the minimum and the maximum boundaries of regulation within which a specific rule is set at the local level.

Consequently the answer to the question raised above may be as follows: the level of labour rights of Soviet citizens working at joint enterprises may be *higher* as compared with the conditions of work at Soviet enterprises because it does not contradict the Soviet legislation and the national legal regime of labour regulation in the USSR.

As regards exemptions from this regime for foreign citizens, which relate to the pay for work, leaves and pensions, they have a socio-economic nature rather than the legal one. Work at joint enterprises in the territory of the USSR apparently should not lead to a considerable decrease in these essential conditions of labour as compared with the conditions under which they worked previously.

It is also important to take into consideration the great socio-economic differences which exist in such differing systems as socialism and capitalism. Thus for instance the level of pay for work in Western countries is somewhat higher than that of workers having the same trade and qualification in the USSR, but Soviet workers receive considerably higher social benefits from social consumption funds. It is also well known that as compared with capitalist countries the USSR has lower apartment rent, free education, free medical care and other benefits.

Consequently, paying Soviet and foreign citizens working at joint enterprises equal wages for equal work in terms of quantity and quality would mean placing the latter in a less advantageous (actually unequal) position as compared with the former. In fact, inequality in this case (that is differences in some labour conditions) ensures actual equality and represents thereby one of the legal mechanisms for realizing the principle of social equality. It is this principle that serves as the criterion which was chosen by Soviet law-makers with a view to determining the correlation between the general and the particular in legal regulation of labour of Soviet and foreign citizens at joint enterprises.

However, it seems that there is another criterion: the optimal efficiency of the joint enterprise. Exemptions from legal regulation of labour common for Soviet and foreign citizens should not hamper attainment of optimal production output by a joint enterprise. Therefore it is precisely for this reason that such essential conditions of labour as the routine of work cannot be excluded, under Decree 49, from the general legal regime and become the object of individual legal regulation between an enterprise and a foreign citizen.

Legal regulation of labour at joint enterprises is still at the stage of inception. At present the number of questions still exceeds the number of available answers. This is quite natural and understandable, simply because such enterprises are a qualitatively new phenomenon for the Soviet national economy. Law-makers are still trying to find the most effective and proper decisions, studying emerging practice and analyzing the experience of other states. There is an evident tendency towards a greater role of the joint enterprise in settling questions of hire and dismissal of workers, the forms and sizes of wages and also of material incentives paid in Soviet currency to those engaged at the joint enterprise. It is necessary to work out and adopt corresponding legal solutions to such labour relations at joint enterprises as labour contracts (hire, transfer and dismissal of employees), participation of employees in the management of the enterprise, labour discipline, material responsibility, protection of labour, labour disputes and the like.

At present it is extremely important to determine the basic points and main approaches to legal regulation of labour at such enterprises. An attempt to analyze some of these has been undertaken in this chapter.

NOTES

[1] *Comments on the Labour Legislation* (Moscow, 1987), p. 14 (in Russian).
[2] *Vedomosti Verkhovnogo Soveta SSSR*, Art. 836, No. 26, 1981.
[3] 'Centralized' regulation means legal regulation of labour relations by means of elaboration and adoption of corresponding standards at bodies which are superior in relation to the given enterprise; whereas 'local' regulation means establishment of labour conditions within the framework of collective labour relations (as a rule under an agreement between the management and the trade-union committee of the enterprise) at the level of the enterprise.

1991 SUPPLEMENTARY COMMENTARY

To date the practice of creating JEs in the Soviet Union has shown that an insignificant number of foreign citizens work in such enterprises. On the whole the labour collectives of such enterprises are formed by Soviet citizens. An analysis of activities of Soviet–American JEs created between 1987 and 1990 has shown that the number of foreign personnel was relatively insignificant – they comprised only approximately 2 per cent of all employees. On the whole they were managers and employees in higher echelons. In the future, to the extent that largescale industrial JEs are created, the situation may change. But until now legal regulations have in practice been intended to apply to employees who are Soviet citizens.

Soviet legislation adopted in 1991 provides that labour relations in

JEs, including the issues of hiring and dismissal, regimes of work and leisure, conditions of salary and compensation guarantees, are regulated by collective agreements and individual employment agreements.

The principal rule of legislation is that the terms and conditions of employment (whether under a collective or individual employment agreement) may not be *less favourable* than those provided under legislation of the republic where the enterprise is created.

Independent trade unions may also now be created at joint enterprises. Their activities must conform to Soviet legislation.

The social insurance of employees of enterprises with foreign investment, and their social security (except for pensions of foreign workers), is regulated by norms of legislation in force in the respective republics. Pension payments for foreign workers in such enterprises are transferred to the respective funds of the countries of their permanent place of residence, in the currencies of and upon the conditions prescribed by such countries. These enterprises deposit state social insurance deductions for Soviet and foreign workers, and pension deductions for Soviet workers, at the rates established for Soviet enterprises and organizations.

Appendix 1

ON THE PROCEDURE FOR THE CREATION ON THE TERRITORY OF THE USSR AND THE ACTIVITIES OF JOINT ENTERPRISES WITH THE PARTICIPATION OF SOVIET ORGANIZATIONS AND FIRMS OF CAPITALIST AND DEVELOPING COUNTRIES (DECREE 49)

[Decree of the USSR Council of Ministers adopted 13 January 1987, No. 49. *SP SSSR* (1987), No. 9, item 40; as amended by Decrees No. 352 of 17 March 1988, No. 385 of 6 May 1989, No. 574 of 20 July 1989, No. 780 of 6 August 1990 and No. 884 of 3 September 1990. *Svod zakonov SSSR*, IX, 50–19; *SP SSSR* (1989), No. 23, item 75; No. 28, item 106; (1990), No. 19, item 100; No. 26, item 121. © Translation Copyright by Professor W. E. Butler SBL.]

With a view to the further development of trade, economic, scientific and technical cooperation with capitalist and developing countries on a stable and mutually advantageous basis, the Council of Ministers of the USSR decrees:

I. *General Provisions*

1. To establish that joint enterprises with the participation of Soviet organizations and firms of capitalist and developing countries (hereinafter 'joint enterprises') shall be created on the territory of the USSR on the basis of contracts concluded by participants of such enterprises [as amended by Decree No. 352, 17 March 1988].

Joint enterprises shall be guided in their activities by the Edict of the Presidium of the USSR Supreme Soviet of 13 January 1987 'On questions connected with the creation on the territory of the USSR and the activities of joint enterprises, international associations, and organizations with the participation of Soviet and foreign organizations, firms and agencies of administration' [*Vedomosti SSSR* (1987), No. 2, item 35], by the present decree and by other acts of legislation of the USSR and Union republics, with the exceptions established by inter-state and intergovernmental treaties of the USSR.

2. Proposals concerning the creation of joint enterprises shall,

together with the technical and economic substantiation and draft constitutive documents, be submitted by the interested Soviet organizations to the agency of administration with whose consent the joint enterprise is created [as amended 6 May 1989].

[Secret section, repealed by Decree No. 352, 17 March 1988.]

Decisions on the creation of joint enterprises with firms of capitalist and developing countries shall be adopted by state enterprises, associations and organizations with the consent of the superior agency of administration [as amended by Decree No. 385, 6 May 1989].

Cooperatives effectuating production activities shall create joint enterprises with the participation of foreign organizations and firms with the consent respectively of the council of ministers of a Union republic which is not divided into regions, the autonomous republic council of ministers, the territory executive committee, regional executive committee, Moscow city executive committee, or Leningrad city executive committee at the place where the cooperative is located, or with the consent of the ministry (or department) with whose enterprise (or organization, institution) the cooperative has been founded [added by Decree No. 385, 6 May 1989].

New construction or largescale conversion when creating joint enterprises shall be effectuated with the consent of territorial agencies of administration [added by Decree No. 385, 6 May 1989].

In other instances the Soviet participants of joint enterprises shall submit the respective information to the territorial agencies of administration [added by Decree No. 385, 6 May 1989].

3. Ministries and departments within whose system the Soviet participants of joint enterprises are situated shall, when creating such enterprises, have as their purpose the fuller satisfaction of the requirements of the country for specific types of industrial products, raw materials and foodstuffs, the attraction to the national economy of the USSR of progressive foreign technology, management experience and additional material and financial resources, the development of the export base of the country, and the reduction of irrational imports.

[Secret section.]

II. *Participants, Property, and Rights of Joint Enterprises*

4. One or several Soviet enterprises (or associations and other organizations) who are juridical persons and one or several foreign firms (or companies, corporations and other organizations) who are juridical persons may be participants of a joint enterprise.

5. The share of the Soviet and foreign participants in the charter fund of a joint enterprise shall be determined by arrangement between them [as amended by Decree No. 385, 6 May 1989].

6. Joint enterprises shall be juridical persons according to Soviet legislation. They may conclude contracts in their own name, acquire property and personal non-property rights, and bear duties, and be plaintiffs or defendants in a court or arbitration tribunal. Joint enterprises shall have an independent balance sheet and operate on the basis of full economic accountability, non-subsidy and self-financing.

7. A joint enterprise must have a charter confirmed by its participants. The charter shall determine the object and purposes of the activities of the enterprise, its location, the composition of the participants, the amount of the charter fund, the amount of the share of the participants, the procedure for forming the charter fund (including in foreign currency), the structure, composition, and competence of the agencies of administration of the enterprise, the procedure for adopting decisions and the range of issues whose decision requires unanimity, as well as the procedure for liquidating the enterprise. Other provisions also may be included in the charter which are not contrary to Soviet legislation and which appertain to the peculiarities of the activities of the joint enterprise.

8. The period of activity of a joint enterprise shall be agreed by the participants in the contract creating the enterprise or in the charter thereof (hereinafter 'constitutive documents').

9. Joint enterprises created on the territory of the USSR shall, after the entry into force of their constitutive documents, be registered at the USSR Ministry of Finances and shall acquire the rights of a juridical person from the moment of registration. Notice of the creation of joint enterprises shall be published in the press.

10. The charter fund of a joint enterprise shall be formed from contributions of the participants thereof. It may be augmented by profits from the economic activities of the enterprise and, when necessary, also by additional contributions from the participants thereof.

11. Buildings, installations, equipment and other material valuables, rights to use land, water and other natural resources, buildings, installations, equipment, and also other property rights (including to use inventions or know-how) and cash in the currencies of participant-countries of the joint enterprise or in a freely-convertible currency may be contributed to the charter fund of a joint enterprise.

12. The contribution of a Soviet participant to the charter fund of a joint enterprise shall be valued by arrangement with the foreign participant both in Soviet and also in foreign currency according to contract prices, taking into account world market prices. The contribution of a foreign participant shall be valued in the same procedure, the value of the contribution being converted into roubles according to the official exchange rate of the State Bank of the USSR on the date of signing the contract concerning the creation of the joint enterprise or other date agreed by the participants thereof. In the absence of world market prices, the value of contributed property shall be determined by agreement between the participants [as amended by Decree No. 352, 17 March 1988].

13. Equipment, materials and other property imported to the USSR by foreign participants of a joint enterprise as their contributions to the charter fund of the enterprise shall be exempted from the payment of customs duty.

Goods imported into the USSR by a joint enterprise for production development needs may be levied with the minimum duty or exempted from the payment of duty [added by Decree No. 385, 6 May 1989].

14. The property of a joint enterprise shall be subject to compulsory insurance at insurance agencies of the USSR.

The risks of joint enterprises shall be insured by agreement of the parties [added by Decree No. 385, 6 May 1989].

15. A joint enterprise shall exercise, in accordance with Soviet legislation, the possession, use and disposition of its property in accordance with the purpose of its activities and purpose of the property. Its property shall not be subject to requisition or confiscation in an administrative proceeding.

The property rights of a joint enterprise shall be subject to being protected in accordance with the provision of Soviet legislation established for Soviet state organizations. Execution may be levied against the property of joint enterprises only by decision of the agencies which in accordance with legislation of the USSR may consider disputes with the participation of joint enterprises.

16. The participants of a joint enterprise shall have the right by mutual consent to transfer their share in the joint enterprise wholly or partially to third persons [as amended by Decree No. 352, 17 March 1988, and Decree No. 385, 6 May 1989].

The Soviet participants shall have a preferential right to acquire the shares of the foreign participants. [Paragraph 2 was repealed by Decree No. 352, 17 March 1988.]

When a joint enterprise is reorganized, its rights and obligations shall pass to the legal successors.

17. The rights to industrial property which belongs to joint enterprises shall be protected in accordance with Soviet legislation, including in the form of patents. The procedure for the transfer of industrial property rights to a joint enterprise by its participants and by a joint enterprise to its participants, as well as the commercial use of such rights and the protection thereof abroad, shall be determined by the constitutive documents.

18. A joint enterprise shall be liable for its obligations with all the property which belongs to it.

The Soviet state and the participants of a joint enteprise shall not be liable for its obligations, and the joint enterprise shall not be liable for the obligations of the Soviet state and of its participants.

Branches of joint enterprises which are created on the territory of the USSR and which are juridical persons shall not be liable for the obligations of joint enterprises, and joint enterprises shall not be liable for the obligations of such branches.

19. Joint enterprises created on the territory of the USSR may open branches and representations if the constitutive documents have granted this right to them.

Branches of joint enterprises created with the participation of Soviet organizations on the territory of other countries shall be opened on the territory of the USSR in the procedure established for the creation of joint enterprises.

20. The disputes of joint enterprises with Soviet state, cooperative and other social organizations, disputes between themselves, as well as disputes between the participants of a joint enterprise regarding issues connected with the activities thereof, shall be considered in accordance with USSR legislation in the courts of the USSR or, by arrangement of the parties, in an arbitration tribunal.

III. *Procedure for Activities of Joint Enterprises*

21. The highest agency of a joint enterprise shall be the board, consisting of persons appointed by the participants thereof. The procedure for the adoption of decisions by the board shall be determined by the constitutive documents.

The direction of current activities of a joint enterprise shall be effectuated by a directorate formed from Soviet and foreign citizens.

The chairman of the board or director-general of a joint enterprise may be either a Soviet or a foreign citizen. A foreign citizen may hold only one of the said posts [as amended 6 May 1989].

Questions of principle of the activity of a joint enterprise shall be decided at sessions of the board on the basis of unanimity of all members of the board [added by Decree No. 385, 6 May 1989].

22. A joint enterprise shall enter into relations with the central agencies of state administration of the USSR and Union republics through agencies superior to the Soviet participant of this enterprise, and with local agencies of administration and other Soviet organizations directly.

23. A joint enterprise shall independently work out and confirm the programme of its economic activities. State agencies of the USSR shall not establish binding planning tasks for a joint enterprise, and the sale of its products shall not be guaranteed.

24. A joint enterprise shall be granted the right to conduct export and import operations independently which are necessary for its economic activities, including operations on the markets of CMEA member countries.

The said export and import operations may also be performed through Soviet foreign trade organizations or the sale network of foreign participants on the basis of respective contracts.

A joint enterprise shall have the right to carry on correspondence, telegraph, teletype and telephone communications with the organizations of other countries. [Paragraph 3 lost force pursuant to Decree No. 574, 20 July 1989.]

25. All currency expenditures of a joint enterprise, including the payment of profit and other amounts due foreign participants and specialists, must be ensured by the joint enterprise from receipts from the realization of its products on the foreign market.

26. The procedure for the realization of products of a joint enterprise on the Soviet market and the delivery to the joint enterprise from this market of equipment, raw materials, materials, component manufactures, fuel, power and other products, as well as the type of currency connected with accounts for the realization of the product and goods purchased, shall be determined by the joint enterprise by agreement with the Soviet enterprises and organizations [as amended by Decree No. 352, 17 March 1988].

27. A joint enterprise may, when necessary, use credits obtained on commercial terms:

in foreign currency: at the Foreign Trade Bank of the USSR or, with the consent of the Foreign Trade Bank of the USSR, at foreign banks or firms;

in roubles: at the State Bank of the USSR or at the Foreign Trade Bank of the USSR.

28. The State Bank of the USSR and the Foreign Trade Bank of the USSR shall have the right to effectuate control over the designated use, provision and timely repayment of credits issued to the joint enterprise.

29. The cash assets of a joint enterprise shall be deposited in its rouble or currency account respectively at the State Bank of the USSR or the Foreign Trade Bank of the USSR and shall be spent for purposes connected with the activities of the enterprise. A joint enterprise shall be credited with interest on the amounts deposited in its accounts:

in foreign currency: by proceeding from world money market rates;

in roubles: on the terms and in the procedure determined by the State Bank of the USSR.

Exchange rate differences with respect to the currency accounts of joint enterprises, as well as with regard to their operations in a foreign currency, shall be relegated to their profits and losses.

30. A reserve fund and other funds needed for the activities thereof and for the social development of the collective shall be created at a joint enterprise.

Deductions from profits for the reserve fund shall be made so long as that fund does not reach 25 per cent of the charter fund of the enterprise. The amounts of annual deductions shall be determined in the procedure established by the constitutive documents.

The list of other funds and the procedure for forming and spending them shall be determined in the constitutive documents.

31. The profit of a joint enterprise, deducting the amounts regarding mutual relations with the state budget of the USSR and amounts directed toward the creation and replenishment of funds, shall be distributed between the participants thereof in proportion to the share participation in the charter fund.

32. The transfer abroad in foreign currency of the amounts due them as a result of the distribution of profits from enterprise activities shall be guaranteed to foreign participants.

33. Joint enterprises shall make amortization deductions in accordance with the prescriptions in force for Soviet state organizations unless provided otherwise in the constitutive documents. The amounts set aside shall remain at the disposal of the joint enterprises.

34. The designing and capital construction of installations of joint enterprises, including objects of social designation, shall be effectuated under contracts from its own and from borrowed assets. Prior to their confirmation designs shall be subject to agreement in the procedure established by the State Construction Committee of the USSR. The quotas of construction and assembly work to be fulfilled by Soviet construction and assembly organizations and the material resources needed for construction shall, upon the orders of joint enterprises, be allocated by way of priority.

35. The carriage of goods of joint enterprises shall be effectuated in the procedure established for Soviet organizations.

IV. *Taxation of Joint Enterprises*

36. Joint enterprises shall pay a tax in the amount of 30 per cent of that portion of the profit left after deductions for the reserve fund, as well as for other funds of the joint enterprise earmarked for the development of production, science and technology. The tax shall be credited to the revenues of the Union budget.

Joint enterprises shall be exempt from the payment of a tax on profit during the first two years from the moment of receiving a declared profit [as amended by Decree No. 352, 17 March 1988].

The USSR Ministry of Finances shall have the right to reduce the amount of the tax or to wholly exempt individual payers from the tax.

37. The tax on profit shall be calculated by the joint enterprise.

An advance amount of the tax for the current year shall be determined by the enterprise, taking into account the financial plan for the current year.

The final amount of the tax on profit actually received during the preceding calendar year shall be calculated by the joint enterprise not later than 15 March of the following year.

38. Tax agencies shall have the right to verify the correctness of the calculation of the tax by joint enterprises [as amended 3 September 1990].

Excess payments of the tax for the past year may be credited to current payments of the tax or refunded to the payer at the application thereof.

39. The amount of tax on profit for the current year shall be paid in to the budget in equal shares not later than 15 days after the expiration of each quarter. The final amount of the tax shall be paid not later than 1 April of the following year.

A penalty in the amount of 0.005 per cent for each day of delay shall be recovered for delay of payment.

Amounts of tax not paid within the period shall be recovered in accordance with the Statute on the Recovery of Taxes and Non-Tax Payments Not Made Within the Period, confirmed by Edict of the Presidium of the USSR Supreme Soviet of 26 January 1981 (*Vedomosti SSSR* (1981), no. 5, item 122) [as amended 3 September 1990].

40. A joint enterprise shall have the right to appeal against the actions of tax agencies connected with the recovery of tax. The application shall be filed at the tax agency which verified the calculation of tax. A decision with regard to it shall be rendered within a month from the date of receiving the application [as amended 3 September 1990].

The decision regarding the application may be appealed, within a month, to the superior tax agency [as amended 3 September 1990].

The filing of an appeal shall not suspend the payment of the tax.

41. Unless provided otherwise by a treaty between the USSR and respective foreign state, the portion of the profit due to a foreign participant of a joint enterprise shall, when transferred abroad, be levied with a tax in the amount of 20 per cent.

The USSR Ministry of Finances shall have the right to reduce the amount of tax on the portion of profit due to a foreign participant of a joint enterprise when it is transferred abroad or to fully exempt it from this tax for a specified period [added by Decree No. 385, 6 May 1989].

42. The said procedure of taxation shall extend to revenues obtained by joint enterprises created on the territory of the USSR and by branches of joint enterprises situated in the USSR and created with the participation of Soviet organizations in other countries from activities both on the territory of the USSR, on the continental shelf and in the economic zone of the USSR, and also on the territory of other countries.

43. An instruction on the taxation of joint enterprises shall be promulgated by the USSR Ministry of Finances.

V. *Control of Activities of Joint Enterprises*

44. Data affecting the activities of the enterprise and the state of its property, profits and losses shall be provided for the purpose of exercising rights of control to the participants of the joint enterprise in the procedure provided by the constitutive documents.

The audits of the financial and economic activities of a joint enterprise shall be carried out by agreement of the parties [added by Decree No. 385, 6 May 1989].

A joint enterprise may have an audit commission formed in the procedure provided by the constitutive documents.

45. Joint enterprises shall keep operational, book-keeping and statistical records in the procedure prevailing in the USSR for Soviet state enterprises. The forms for such records and reports shall be confirmed by the USSR Ministry of Finances jointly with the Central Statistical Administration of the USSR.

Joint enterprises shall bear responsibility in accordance with Soviet legislation for the observance of the procedure for keeping and for the reliability of the records and reports.

Joint enterprises may not provide any reports and information to agencies of foreign states [as amended by Decree No. 385, 6 May 1989].

46. The verification of financial, economic and commercial activities of joint enterprises for the purposes of determining the correctness of tax levies shall be effectuated for a fee by a Soviet economically-accountable auditing organization [as amended 6 May 1989].

VI. *Personnel of Joint Enterprises*

47. The personnel of joint enterprises shall be made up principally of Soviet citizens. The administration of a joint enterprise shall be obliged to conclude collective contracts with the trade union organization created at the enterprise. The contents of such contracts, including the provisions of the social development of the collective, shall be determined by Soviet legislation and the constitutive documents.

48. The work and leisure regime for Soviet citizens who are working at joint enterprises, and their social security and social insurance, shall be regulated by norms of Soviet legislation. These norms shall extend to foreign citizens who are working at joint enterprises except for issues of payment of labour, granting of leave, and pension security resolved by contract with each foreign citizen. Joint enterprises shall independently decide questions of the form and amounts for payment of labour and material incentive in Soviet roubles, as well as questions of hiring and dismissal and other labour

conditions while observing the rights of citizens provided by Soviet legislative acts [as amended 6 May 1989].

The State Committee of the USSR for Labour and Social Matters and the All-Union Central Trade Union Council shall have the right to determine the peculiarities of the application of Soviet legislation concerning social insurance for foreign citizens who are working at joint enterprises.

49. A joint enterprise shall pay to the state budget of the USSR deductions for state social insurance of Soviet and foreign workers and deductions for the pension security of Soviet workers at the rates established for Soviet state organizations. Payments for the pension security of foreign workers of a joint enterprise shall be remitted to the respective funds of the countries of their permanent place of residence (in the currency of those countries).

50. The unspent portion of these earnings may be transferred abroad in foreign currency [redaction per Decree No. 780, 6 August 1990].

VII. *Liquidation of Joint Enterprises*

51. A joint enterprise may be liquidated in the instances and in the procedure provided for by the constitutive documents, and also by decision of the USSR Council of Ministers, if its activities do not correspond to the purposes and tasks provided for in those documents. Notice of the liquidation of a joint enterprise shall be published in the press.

52. A foreign participant shall, in the event of the liquidation of a joint enterprise or of his withdrawal therefrom, receive the right to the return of his contribution in cash or in the form of goods in accordance with the remaining value of the contribution at the moment of liquidation of the enterprise after payment of his obligations to Soviet participants and third persons.

53. The liquidation of a joint enterprise shall be registered at the Ministry of Finances of the USSR.

Appendix 2

LAW ON THE GENERAL PRINCIPLES OF ENTREPRENEURSHIP OF CITIZENS IN THE USSR

[Adopted by the USSR Supreme Soviet, 2 April 1991. *Pravda*, 11 April 1991, p. 2, cols. 1–7. © Translation Copyright 1991 by Professor W. E. Butler SBL.]

The present law determines the general principles of entrepreneurship in the USSR, regulates the rights and responsibility of subjects of entrepreneurial activities, ensures state protection and support for them, and regulates relations of entrepreneurs with agencies of state administration.

The law is directed towards the creation of conditions for the extensive display of economic initiative and entrepreneurialness of citizens on the basis of realizing the principle of equality of all forms of ownership, the freedom to dispose of property and choice of sphere of activity.

1. *Entrepreneurship*

Entrepreneurship (or entrepreneurial activity) is the initiative, autonomous activity of citizens directed towards receiving profit or personal revenue, effectuated in their own names, at their own risk, and under their own property responsibility or in the name of and under the property responsibility of a juridical person–enterprise.

An entrepreneur may effectuate any types of economic activity unless they are prohibited by legislative acts of the USSR and republics, including commercial intermediary commodity-purchase, innovatory, advisory, and other activity, as well as operations with securities.

2. *Legislation on Entrepreneurship*

Relations connected with entrepreneurship, irrespective of the forms of ownership, type and sphere of activity, shall be regulated by the Fundamental Principles of Civil Legislation, the present law and other legislative acts of the USSR and republics.

If in order to effectuate entrepreneurial activity an enterprise which is a juridical person is created or acquired by the entrepreneur, its activity shall also be regulated by the USSR Law on Enterprises in the USSR and by other legislation on enterprises unless provided otherwise by the present law.

The peculiarities of entrepreneurial activity of foreign citizens, including with respect to the acquisition of the property of state enterprises, also shall be regulated by legislation of the USSR and republics on foreign investments on the territory of the USSR.

In relations where foreign natural or juridical persons are one of the parties, the rules of an international treaty shall apply if other rules have been established by the latter than those which are contained in legislation of the USSR with regard to questions of entrepreneurial activity.

3. *Subjects of Entrepreneurship*

There may engage in entrepreneurship:

any citizen of the USSR who is not restricted in rights in the .procedure determined by legislative acts of the USSR and republics;

any foreign citizen or stateless person, except for instances provided for by legislative acts of the USSR and republics;

a group of citizens (or partners) – a collective of entrepreneurs.

The engaging in entrepreneurial activity by executive workers and specialists of state agencies within whose functions are the deciding of questions connected with the effectuation of entrepreneurial activity or control over such activity shall not be permitted.

4. *Forms of Entrepreneurship*

The forms of entrepreneurship shall be private entrepreneurship and collective entrepreneurship effectuated by subjects of entrepreneurship on the basis of the ownership of citizens, as well as property and used on legal grounds.

The state shall recognize any forms of entrepreneurship effectuated within the framework of the law and socially useful activity and shall ensure the legal guarantees and support thereof.

Entrepreneurship may be effectuated within the limits established by legislation of the USSR and republics:

without the use of hired labour;

with the use of hired labour;

without the formation of a juridical person;

with the formation of a juridical person.

A special form of entrepreneurial activity shall be entrepreneurial activity effectuated by the director of an enterprise if he is under a contract with the owner of the property of the enterprise or a person (or agency) empowered by him has been endowed with all the rights and duties and bears the responsibility established by the present law for an entrepreneur.

5. *Rights of Entrepreneur*

An entrepreneur shall have the right to:

create, in order to effectuate its activity, any types of enterprise or organization which are not contrary to legislative acts of the USSR and republics;

acquire wholly or partially the property of state enterprises and enterprises based on other forms of ownership, other property, and property rights;

participate with his property and with property received on legal grounds in the activity of other economic subjects;

use by agreement of the parties the property of juridical persons and citizens;

hire and dismiss workers on the conditions of a contract and on other conditions established by legislation;

autonomously establish the forms, system and amounts of the payment of labour and other types of revenues of persons hired;

autonomously form the programme of economic activity, choose the suppliers and consumers of the product (or work, services) produced, and fulfil work and deliveries for state needs on a contractual basis;

establish prices and tariffs in accordance with legislative acts of the USSR and republics;

open accounts in banks in order to keep cash assets and to effectuate all types of account, credit and cashier operations;

freely dispose of profit (or revenue) from entrepreneurial activity remaining after the payment of taxes and making other compulsory payments. When effectuating entrepreneurial activity on the basis of a contract, the procedure for the distribution of profit shall be regulated by this contract;

receive any personal revenue without limitation of amount;

use in the procedure established by law the state social security and social insurance system;

appeal in the established procedure the actions of state and other agencies which impinge upon his rights or legal interests;

act as a participant of foreign economic relations in the procedure established by legislation for juridical persons;

effectuate currency operations in the procedure established by the USSR Law on Currency Regulation.

6. *Duties and Responsibility of Entrepreneur*

An entrepreneur shall be obliged to:

conclude contracts with citizens hired for work, as well as, when necessary, collective contracts with trade unions acting in the name of labour collectives, in accordance with legislation of the USSR and republics. An entrepreneur shall not have the right to obstruct the combining of hired workers into the trade unions in order to defend their socio-economic interests;

effectuate the payment of labour for hired persons at a level not lower than the minimum amounts established by legislative acts of the USSR and republics;

make deductions to the State Social Insurance Fund regarding the insurance of hired persons in the procedure and in the amounts established by legislation of the USSR and republics;

provide to hired persons conditions of labour in accordance with legislation and the contracts concluded;

effectuate measures relating to ensuring ecological security, labour protection, safety, production hygiene and sanitation, being guided by prevailing statutes and norms;

comply with the rights and legal interests of consumers and ensure the proper quality of goods (or work, services) produced;

receive a special authorization (or licence) for activity in the spheres which are subject to licensing in accordance with legislation of the USSR and republics.

An entrepreneur effectuating his activities without the formation of a juridical person shall be liable for his obligations connected with this activity with all of his property, except for that property against which in accordance with legislative acts of the republics execution may not be levied.

An entrepreneur effectuating his activity on the basis of a contract shall be liable for the obligations of the enterprise directed by him with all of his property, except for that property against which in accordance with legislation of the republics execution may not be levied. He shall bear the same responsibility for the failure to perform or for the improper performance of obligations arising from the contract.

7. State Registration of Citizens Engaging in Entrepreneurial Activity Without Formation of Juridical Person

The state registration of citizens who are engaging in entrepreneurial activity without the formation of a juridical person shall be effectuated in the procedure determined by legislation of the USSR and republics.

8. Termination of Entrepreneurial Activity

The termination of entrepreneurial activity shall be effectuated by the decision of the entrepreneur or a court.

Entrepreneurial activity shall be terminated by a court in instances of:

deeming an entrepreneur to be bankrupt;

repeated or flagrant violation of legislation;

effectuation by an entrepreneur of activity in which it is prohibited to engage, or activity requiring the receipt of special authorization (or licence) without such authorization;

violation of norms of ecological security;

on other grounds provided for by legislative acts of the republics.

A court which has adopted a decision concerning the termination of entrepreneurial activity in the instances established by the present article shall determine the procedure and periods for the termination of entrepreneurial activity in accordance with legislative acts of the USSR and republics.

In the event of the death of the entrepreneur, his rights and duties regarding the effectuation of entrepreneurial activity shall pass to his heirs.

Entrepreneurial activity effectuated on the basis of a contract may be terminated upon the expiry of the term of this contract or its dissolution upon the application of one of the parties in the instances and procedure provided for by the contract.

9. Taxation of Profit from Entrepreneurial Activity and Personal Revenue of Entrepreneur

Profit from entrepreneurial activity effectuated with the formation of a juridical person shall be taxed in the procedure established for the taxation of enterprises by the USSR Law on Taxes from Enterprises,

Associations and Organizations. The taxation of personal revenue of an entrepreneur in this event shall be effectuated in the procedure established by the USSR Law on Income Tax from Citizens of the USSR, Foreign Citizens and Stateless Persons.

10. *State Support of Entrepreneurship*

The state shall guarantee compliance with the rights and legal interests of the entrepreneur, create conditions for free good-faith competition of entrepreneurs, ensure them equal opportunities of access to material-thing, financial, labour, informational and natural resources without allowing the monopolization of the market for those resources.

In order to enhance the effectiveness and extensive dissemination of entrepreneurial activity, the state shall create conditions for the direct support of entrepreneurship, including informational, advisory, scientific and instructional centres, as well as innovation and insurance funds.

11. *Protection of Rights of Entrepreneurs*

If as a result of the publication of an act by a state or other agency which does not correspond to its competence or the requirements of legislation the rights of an entrepreneur are violated, he shall have the right to apply to a court to deem such an act to be void.

Losses caused to an entrepreneur, including lost advantage, as a result of the fulfilment of the instructions of state or other agencies or their officials which violated the right of an entrepreneur, and also as a consequence of the improper effectuation by such agencies or officials of duties with respect to the entrepreneur provided for by legislation, shall be subject to compensation by those agencies.

Disputes concerning compensation of losses shall be decided by a court.

DECREE ON THE INTRODUCTION INTO EFFECT OF THE LAW OF THE USSR ON THE GENERAL PRINCIPLES OF ENTREPRENEURSHIP OF CITIZENS IN THE USSR

[Decree of the USSR Supreme Soviet, 4 April 1991. *Pravda*, 11 April 1991, p. 2, cols. 1–7. © Translation Copyright 1991 by Professor W.E. Butler SBL.]

The USSR Supreme Soviet decrees:

1. To introduce the Law of the USSR on the General Principles of Entrepreneurship of Citizens in the USSR into effect from the moment of publication.

2. Prevailing acts of legislation which are not contrary to the said law shall be applied until legislation of the USSR and republics is brought into conformity with the Law of the USSR on General Principles of Entrepreneurship of Citizens in the USSR.

3. Until the adoption by the republics of legislation on the procedure for state registration of entrepreneurs effectuating their activity without the formation of a juridical person, such registration shall be effectuated without the recovery of payment by the executive committees of district, city or district in city soviets of people's deputies at the place of residence of the entrepreneur in accordance with a temporary procedure confirmed by the USSR Council of Ministers.

4. The USSR Council of Ministers shall:

submit for consideration at the current session of the USSR Supreme Soviet proposals concerning the bringing of legislative acts of the USSR into accordance with the Law of the USSR on General Principles of Entrepreneurship of Citizens in the USSR;

bring decrees and regulations of the government of the USSR into accordance with the said law before 1 June 1991;

ensure before 1 June 1991 the review and repeal by ministries and departments of the USSR of their normative acts which are contrary to the said law;

work out before 1 January 1992 the all-Union programme for promoting the development of entrepreneurial activity of citizens, providing therein in particular measures of state support for those types of entrepreneurial activity which are directed towards the improvement of the health protection of the populace, enhancing ecological security and environmental protection, and increasing the production of food products and consumer goods;

analyze before 1 June 1991 the course of the fulfilment of the Decree of the USSR Council of Ministers of 8 August 1990, No. 790, 'On measures relating to the creation and development of small enterprises' and take necessary decisions on the basis thereof.

5. To deem to have lost force the Law of the USSR on Individual Labour Activity of 19 November 1986 [*Vedomosti SSSR* (1986), No. 47, item 964; (1988), No. 11, item 174] from the moment of the

introduction into effect of the USSR Law on General Principles of Entrepreneurship of Citizens in the USSR.

Citizens effectuating their activity on the basis of the USSR Law on Individual Labour Activity must undergo registration in the procedure provided for by the present decree before 1 January 1992. Patents and registration certificates issued to citizens on the grounds and in the procedure established by the USSR Law on Individual Labour Activity shall retain their force during 1991.

Until changes are made in the USSR Law on Income Tax from Citizens of the USSR, Foreign Citizens and Stateless Persons for entrepreneurs effectuating their activity without the formation of a juridical person, the operation of Article 19(2), Article 20 and Article 21 of the said law shall be extended.

Appendix 3

FUNDAMENTAL PRINCIPLES OF LEGISLATION ON FOREIGN INVESTMENTS IN THE USSR (FPForInv)

[Adopted by the USSR Supreme Soviet, 5 July 1991. *Izvestiia*, 24 July 1991, p. 4, cols. 1–7. © Translation Copyright Professor W.E. Butler SBL.]

The present FPForInv shall determine the general principles of effectuating foreign investments on the territory of the USSR directed towards ensuring the effective use in the national economy of the USSR of foreign material and financial resources, modern foreign technology, scientific–technical achievements and management experience, and shall guarantee the protection of the rights of foreign investors.

I. *General Provisions*

1. *Legislation on foreign investments of USSR and republics.* Relations connected with foreign investments on the territory of the USSR shall be regulated by legislation of the USSR and republics with the exceptions provided for by the present FPForInv and other legislation of the USSR and republics on foreign investments. Relations connected with foreign investments on their territories shall be regulated by legislation of the republics in accordance with the present FPForInv, taking into account the peculiarities of economic activity and investment policy of the republics, except for relations whose regulation has been relegated to the jurisdiction of the USSR, and also relations the duty to regulate which by the USSR arises from international treaties of the USSR.

2. *Foreign investors.* There may be foreign investors in the USSR:

(*a*) foreign juridical persons;

(*b*) foreign citizens, and also stateless persons and citizens of the USSR having a permanent place of residence abroad;

(*c*) foreign associations not having the rights of a juridical person;

(*d*) foreign states;

(*e*) international organizations.

3. *Foreign investments and forms of effectuating them.* All types of property and property rights, including the rights to the results of intellectual activity and other rights not relating to [rights in] things, contributed by foreign investors to objects of entrepreneurial activity for the purposes of obtaining a profit or the transfer of knowledge shall be foreign investments.

Foreign investors may effectuate investments on the territory of the USSR by means of:

(*a*) share participation in enterprises and organizations jointly with Soviet juridical persons and citizens;

(*b*) the creation of enterprises which belong wholly to foreign investors;

(*c*) the acquisition of property, including stocks and other securities;

(*d*) the acquisition of the rights of use of land and other natural resources, and also other property rights autonomously or with the participation of Soviet juridical persons and citizens;

(*e*) the conclusion of contracts with Soviet juridical persons and citizens providing for other forms of effectuating foreign investments.

4. *Participation of foreign investors in destatization and privatization of enterprises.* Foreign juridical persons and citizens, foreign associations not having the rights of a juridical person, international organizations, and also stateless persons and citizens of the USSR having a permanent place of residence abroad, may participate in destatization and privatization of enterprises in all-Union, republic and municipal ownership on the territory of the USSR.

The said foreign investors may acquire in the established procedure an enterprise (or share) in all-Union ownership with the consent of labour collectives in the event that Soviet subjects refuse to acquire such enterprises (or shares) and with the authorization of the State Property Fund of the USSR.

The conditions of participation of the said investors in destatization and privatization of enterprises in republic and municipal ownership shall be determined by legislation of the republics.

5. *Legal regime of foreign investments.* The legal regime of foreign investments on the territory of the USSR may not be less favourable than the respective regime for property and non-property rights, and

also of the investment activity, of Soviet enterprises, organizations and citizens, with the exceptions provided for by legislative acts of the USSR and republics on foreign investments.

Additional tax and other privileges may be established for foreign investments in priority branches of the economy and for individual territories by legislation of the USSR and republics.

6. *Types of activity.* Foreign investors and enterprises with foreign investments may effectuate any types of activity unless they have been prohibited by legislative acts of the USSR and republics.

Foreign investors and enterprises with foreign investments may engage in individual types of activity, a list of which shall be determined by legislative acts of the USSR and republics, only on the basis of a special authorization (or licence).

7. *Territorial limitations for foreign investments.* Territories on which the activity of foreign investors and enterprises with foreign investments are limited or prohibited may be determined by legislative acts of the USSR and republics by proceeding from considerations of ensuring defence and national security.

8. *State foreign investments agency.* The working out and realization of all-Union policy relating to attracting and using foreign investments, coordination of investment activity, rendering assistance to foreign investors and enterprises with foreign investments in their activities on the territory of the USSR shall be effectuated by a state agency within the jurisdiction of the USSR Council of Ministers, members of which shall be representatives of the republics.

II. *Guarantees of Foreign Investments*

9. *Guarantees against change of legislation.* In the event that subsequent legislation of the USSR and republics worsens the conditions of investing, then the legislation which prevailed at the moment of effectuating the investments shall apply to the foreign investments for ten years.

This provision shall not extend to changes of legislation of the USSR and republics affecting the ensuring of defence, national security and public order; taxation, credits and finances; environmental protection, and the morality and health of the populace; and also anti-monopoly legislation.

10. *Guarantees against nationalization and requisition.* Foreign investments in the USSR shall not be subject to nationalization except

for instances when it is effectuated in accordance with legislative acts of the USSR and republics.

Foreign investments shall not be subject to requisition except for instances of natural calamities, wrecks, epidemics, epizootics and other circumstances of an extraordinary character. Measures relating to requisition shall be adopted by decision of agencies of state power.

Measures relating to nationalization and requisition must not be of a discriminatory character. In the event such measures are adopted, prompt, adequate and effective compensation shall be paid to the foreign investor. It shall be paid without unsubstantiated delay, must correspond to the real value of the investment at the moment the decision concerning nationalization or measures relating to requisition was adopted. Compensation shall be paid in foreign currency and at the wish of the investor may be transferred abroad.

Disputes concerning the amounts of compensation and the periods and procedure for paying it shall be settled in the USSR in courts in accordance with legislative acts of the USSR and republics, and also in an arbitration court if such has been provided for by agreement of the parties or by an international treaty of the USSR.

11. *Guarantees in event of termination of investment activity.* A foreign investor shall, in the event of the termination of investment activity, have the right to compensation of investments due him and revenues received in connection therewith in cash or goods form according to the real value at the moment of terminating investment activity.

12. *Guarantees of transfer of revenues and other amounts in foreign currency.* The transfer abroad of their revenues and other amounts in foreign currency received on legal grounds in connection with investments shall be guaranteed to foreign investors.

13. *Guarantees of use of profits in currency of USSR.* The profit of foreign investors received on the territory of the USSR in the currency of the USSR may be reinvested on the territory of the USSR and used in accordance with legislative acts of the USSR and republics. Foreign investors may have accounts in roubles in empowered banks of the USSR.

Foreign investors may use rouble assets in their accounts for the acquisition of foreign currency at the exchange rates formed within the framework of forms authorized by legislation of the USSR for the purchase and sale of foreign currency for roubles.

III. *Creation and Activity of Enterprises with Foreign Investments*

14. *Enterprises with foreign investments.* By enterprises with foreign investments is understood enterprises with the participation of foreign investors (or joint enterprises) and enterprises belonging wholly to foreign investors.

Enterprises with foreign investments shall be Soviet juridical persons.

Enterprises with foreign investments shall be created in the form of joint stock societies, limited responsibility societies and other economic societies and partnerships, and also in any other forms which are not contrary to legislative acts of the USSR and republics.

A decision concerning the creation of a joint enterprise shall be adopted by its founders autonomously. In the event that the Soviet participant is a state enterprise or an enterprise of a social organization, the decision concerning the creation of the joint enterprise shall be adopted by its founders with the consent of the owner of the property or agency empowered by it.

A decision concerning the creation of an enterprise belonging wholly to a foreign investor shall be adopted in the procedure determined by legislative acts of the republic on whose territory such enterprise is created.

The peculiarities of creating banks with foreign investments shall be established by legislative acts of the USSR on banks and bank activities.

15. *Ecological and sanitary–hygienic expert examination.* When creating an enterprise with foreign investments its founders shall be obliged in the instances and in the procedure provided for by legislation of the USSR and republics to receive the opinion of an expert examination with respect to compliance with sanitary–hygienic and ecological requirements. During the period of activity and at the moment of liquidation an enterprise with foreign investments shall be obliged to obtain such an opinion.

16. *Registration.* An enterprise with foreign investments shall be subject to registration in the procedure established by legislative acts of the republics. Requirements for the constitutive and other documents needed to effectuate registration shall be established by legislation of the USSR and republics.

An enterprise with foreign investments shall acquire the rights of a juridical person from the moment of registration. A communication concerning registration shall be published in the press by the agency effectuating the registration.

Data concerning registration of enterprises with foreign investments shall be included in republic registers and in the unified state register of the USSR, which shall be kept by the state foreign investments agency.

A refusal of registration may be appealed in the USSR in courts.

17. *Branches and representations.* An enterprise with foreign investments may create branches, representations and other solitary subdivisions in the USSR and abroad.

On the territory of the USSR branches, representations and other solitary subdivisions shall not be juridical persons and shall be created while complying with the conditions established by legislation of the USSR and republics for the creation of enterprises.

18. *Subsidiary enterprises.* An enterprise with foreign investments may create subsidiary enterprises in the USSR and abroad.

On the territory of the USSR subsidiary enterprises shall be created as juridical persons in accordance with legislation of the USSR and republics.

19. *Associations of enterprises.* Enterprises with foreign investments may unite into associations [*assotsiatsii*], concerns, consortiums and other associations on the conditions and in the procedure provided for by legislative acts of the USSR and republics. Such enterprises may join associations previously created.

20. *Making of contributions by participants of joint enterprises.* The periods, amount and procedure for making and valuing contributions of each participant to the charter fund of a joint enterprise shall be provided for in the constitutive documents. The value of property contributed by the participants of a joint enterprise as a contribution to the charter fund of an enterprise shall be determined by arrangements between the participants of the joint enterprise.

In the absence, upon the expiry of a year after registration, of documentary confirmation of the fact of each participant paying in 50 per cent of the contributions specified in the constitutive documents to the charter fund, the agency which has registered the said joint enterprise shall deem it to be insolvent and shall exclude it from the register of joint enterprises. Information concerning exclusion from the register shall be published in the press.

21. *Reserve fund.* At enterprises with foreign investments a reserve fund shall be created in an amount of up to 25 per cent of the charter

fund. The formation of the reserve fund shall be effectuated by means of annual deductions both in currency of the USSR and in foreign currency. The amount of annual deductions to the reserve fund and the types of currency shall be determined by the enterprise autonomously.

22. *Realization of product and delivery of territory of USSR.* An enterprise with foreign investments shall have the right on a contractual basis to establish prices for the produce (or work, service) produced by it, determine the procedure for realizing it on the internal market of the USSR, and select suppliers of the produce (or work, services) from this market.

23. *Accounts in foreign currency on territory of USSR.* The use of foreign currency and also payments documents in foreign currency when effectuating accounts on the territory of the USSR by enterprises with foreign investments shall be permitted in the procedure established by legislation of the USSR on currency regulation.

24. *Export and import of product.* Enterprises with foreign investments in whose charter fund foreign investments comprise 15 per cent or more shall have the right to export without licences a product (or work, service) of their own production. An enterprise with foreign investments shall have the right without licences to effectuate the import of the product (or work, service) for its own economic activity.

The procedure for relegating a product (or work, service) to a product of the own production of enterprises with foreign investments shall be established by legislation of the USSR.

25. *Currency receipts.* The currency receipts of an enterprise with foreign investments shall remain at its disposition on condition of complying with legislation of the USSR on currency regulation.

26. *Customs levy.* Property imported into the USSR as the contribution of a foreign investor to the charter fund of a joint enterprise or in order to create an enterprise belonging wholly to a foreign investor shall be exempt from payment of customs duty and shall not be levied with tax on import.

Property imported into the USSR by foreign workers of an enterprise with foreign investments for their own needs shall be exempt from the payment of customs duty.

28. *Insurance.* The insurance of property and risks of an enterprise with foreign investments shall be effectuated at its discretion, unless compulsory insurance has been provided for by legislation of the USSR and republics.

28. *Taxation.* Enterprises with foreign investments, and also foreign investors, shall pay the taxes established by legislative acts of the USSR and republics.

29. *Verification of activity of enterprises with foreign investments.* Tax and other agencies to whom the verification of individual aspects of the activity of enterprises with foreign investments has been entrusted may effectuate such verifications as the need arises and strictly within the limits of their competence. Enterprises shall submit to such agencies respective reports and documentation concerning their activities. Tax and other agencies shall be obliged to ensure the keeping of commercial secrecy.

Verification for the purposes of taxation of financial and commercial activity of such enterprises shall be effectuated by auditor organizations empowered in accordance with legislation of the USSR and republics for carrying on such activity.

30. *Records and reports.* An enterprise with foreign investments shall effectuate operational and book-keeping records and keep statistical reports in accordance with the rules prevailing in the USSR.

31. *Securing obligations.* The property of an enterprise with foreign investments may be used by it in accordance with legislation of the USSR and republics as security for all types of its obligations, including the attraction of borrowed assets. Its property rights to buildings, installations, equipment and other property rights, including the right to use land and other natural resources, also may be security.

32. *Rights to results of intellectual activity and other rights not relating to [rights to] thing.* The protection of rights, provided as foreign investments, to the results of intellectual activity, and also other rights not relating to [the rights to] a thing (know-how, commercial secret, and others) shall be ensured by legislative acts of the USSR and republics.

The use of the results of intellectual activity received at enterprises with foreign investments shall be effectuated in accordance with legislative acts of the USSR and republics.

33. *Labour relations.* Production and labour relations, including questions of hiring and dismissal, the regime of labour and leisure, payment of labour, guarantees and compensation at enterprises with foreign investments shall be regulated by the collective contract (or agreement) and individual labour contracts.

The conditions of collective and individual labour contracts may not worsen the position of workers of that enterprise in comparison with the conditions provided for by legislative acts of the USSR and republics.

Questions of the payment of labour, granting of leaves and the pension security of foreign workers of an enterprise with foreign investments must be decided in individual labour contracts with each of them. The earnings received by such workers in foreign currency may be transferred by them abroad.

34. *Social insurance and security.* Social insurance of workers of an enterprise with foreign investments and the social security thereof (except for pension security of foreign workers) shall be regulated by the norms of Soviet legislation.

An enterprise with foreign investments shall transfer payments for pension security of foreign workers to the respective funds of the countries of their permanent place of residence in the currency of those countries.

An enterprise shall make deductions for state social insurance of Soviet and foreign workers and deductions for the pension security of Soviet workers according to the rates established for Soviet enterprises and organizations.

35. *Liquidation.* An enterprise with foreign investments may be liquidated in the procedure and instances provided for by legislative acts of the USSR and republics.

The accumulated assets of an enterprise with foreign investments shall, when it is liquidated, be subject to taxation at their real value.

IV. *Acquisition of Securities by Foreign Investors*

36. *Acquisition of state securities.* The acquisition by foreign investors of state securities shall be effectuated in the procedure determined by the empowered state agency.

37. *Acquisition of securities of Soviet juridical persons.* Foreign investors shall have the right to acquire stocks and other securities of Soviet juridical persons for foreign currency and currency of the USSR in the procedure and on the conditions determined by legislation of the USSR and republics.

V. *Acquisition by Foreign Investors of Rights to Use Land and Other Property Rights*

38. *Right to use land.* Land, including the lease thereof, may be granted for use to foreign investors and enterprises with foreign

investments in accordance with legislation of the USSR and republics on land.

In the event of the transfer of ownership to a structure or installation, the right to use the land plot shall pass together with those objects in the procedure and on the conditions established by legislation of the republics.

39. *Right to use resources of economic zone of USSR and continental shelf of USSR.* The right to explore, work and exploit the natural resources of the economic zone of the USSR and the continental shelf of the USSR may be granted to foreign investors and enterprises with foreign investments in accordance with legislation of the USSR and republics on the economic zone of the USSR and continental shelf of the USSR.

40. *Lease.* The lease of property to foreign investors and enterprises with foreign investments shall be effectuated by the lessor on the basis of contracts and in accordance with legislative acts of the USSR and republics on lease and lease relations.

41. *Concession contracts.* The granting to foreign investors of concessions for the exploration, working and exploitation of renewable and non-renewable natural resources and for conducting other economic activity shall be effectuated on the basis of concession contracts concluded by foreign investors with empowered agencies of the USSR and republics in the procedure determined by legislative acts of the USSR and republics.

The conditions of effectuating activity of foreign investors shall be determined in the concession contract. Conditions differing from provisions established by legislative acts of the USSR and republics may be contained therein within the limits of the competence respectively of the USSR and republics.

The unilateral change of the conditions of a concession contract shall not be permitted, unless stipulated otherwise in the contract.

VI. *Foreign Investments in Free Economic Zones*

42. *Activity of foreign investors and enterprises with foreign investments in free economic zones.* A territory in which a special regime of economic activity of foreign investors and enterprises with foreign investments is established, and also of Soviet enterprises and citizens, shall be a free economic zone in the USSR.

The procedure for the effectuation of economic activity of foreign investors and enterprises with foreign investments and the conditions of privileged export–import, tax, customs, currency, banking and other types of regulation in each such zone shall be established by legislation of the USSR and republics and by decisions of the respective soviets of people's deputies within the limits of their competence.

A decision concerning the creation of each zone shall be adopted in the procedure established by legislative acts of the republics.

VII. *Concluding Provisions*

43. Consideration of disputes. Disputes between foreign investors and the state shall be subject to consideration in the USSR in courts unless provided otherwise by international treaties of the USSR.

Disputes of foreign investors and of enterprises with foreign investments with Soviet state agencies acting as parties in relations regulated by civil legislation, enterprises, social organizations and other Soviet juridical persons, a dispute between the participants of an enterprise with foreign investments, and also disputes between the participants of an enterprise with foreign investments and the enterprise itself shall be subject to consideration in the USSR in courts or, by arrangement of the parties, by way of arbitration, including abroad, and in the instances provided for by legislative acts of the USSR and republics, in *arbitrazh* courts, economic courts and others.

44. *International treaties.* If other rules have been established by international treaties than those which are contained in legislation of the USSR and republics on foreign investments, the rules of the international treaty shall be applied.

ON THE INTRODUCTION INTO EFFECT OF THE FUNDAMENTAL PRINCIPLES OF LEGISLATION ON FOREIGN INVESTMENTS IN THE USSR

[Decree of the USSR Supreme Soviet, 5 July 1991. *Izvestiia*, 24 July 1991, p. 4, cols. 4–7. © Translation copyright by Professor W.E. Butler SBL.]

The USSR Supreme Soviet decrees:

1. To introduce the Fundamental Principles of Legislation on

Foreign Investments in the USSR into effect from the moment of their publication.

2. The USSR Council of Ministers shall before 1 October 1991:

determine with the participation of the governments of the republics and submit to the USSR Supreme Soviet for confirmation a list of priority branches of the economy, including science, education, public health and culture, and also territories in which it is advisable to grant additional tax and other privileges to foreign investors;

prepare with the participation of the governments of the republics and confirm a Statute on the State Foreign Investments Agency;

work out with the participation of the governments of the republics and confirm the procedure for relegation products (or work, services) to products of own production of enterprises with foreign investments;

determine the state agency for the issuance of state securities and authorize it to work out the procedure and conditions for acquiring such securities by foreign investors;

submit to the USSR Supreme Soviet proposals concerning the bringing of legislative acts of the USSR into conformity with the Fundamental Principles of Legislation on Foreign Investments in the USSR;

bring into conformity with the said FPForInv decisions of the government of the USSR;

ensure the review and repeal by ministries, state committees and departments of the USSR of their normative acts, including instructions, which are contrary to the said FPForInv.

3. The USSR Council of Ministers shall, when deciding practical questions connected with foreign investments, promote the use above all of the work force and material resources of the USSR and republics.

4. The State Bank of the USSR shall work out and introduce into effect the regime for rouble accounts for foreign investors.

5. To establish that:

the procedure for determining the rate of tax on profit provided for by Article 5(3) of the Law of the USSR on Taxes from Enterprises, Associations and Organizations shall not extend to enterprises with foreign investments;

enterprises belonging wholly to foreign investors shall be levied with taxes on the conditions and in the procedure established for joint enterprises, the share of foreign participation in the charter fund of which exceeds 30 per cent.

6. To recommend to the republic supreme soviets to adopt legislative acts on foreign investments and to bring legislation of the republics into conformity with the said FPForInv.